Praise for Shelley Plumb and
To Break or Bounce

"This book is full of imagery that is relatable. The grandmother's advice is priceless. I could hear my grandmother speaking to me as I read the book. *To Break or Bounce* is an easy read that addresses loss, how we deal with it, and how the reader can consider new ways to deal with it. This is also a book about self-care and mental health. A transformational read that is life changing."

—SHANTERA L. CHATMAN, MBA, Founder and Executive Director, The Chatman Women's Foundation, Houston, TX

"Dr. Shelley Plumb's *To Break or Bounce* is a valuable tutorial on how to live a better and richer life. But unlike most tutorials, Dr. Plumb's is as emotional as it is intellectual. From her heart and mind, using both as a GPS, Dr. Plumb guides the reader on a journey to the spirit within. Step by personal step, even through her stumbles, Dr. Plumb shows the readers how to light and nourish the spark, the spirit, that is the core of each of us. Dr. Plumb never claims the journey is easy, but she does maintain throughout that unless we make that journey inward, we will constantly be at the mercy of and buffeted by, the vicissitudes of life. This book could easily have been titled, *Going Inward*, for in her doing so, Dr. Plumb has found the formula for how to bounce and not break from whatever life throws at us. Basically, Dr. Plumb is saying: Stop and smell the roses. For when you do, surprise, surprise, you discover you are your own rosebud just waiting to burst into bloom with your own special beauty."

—ALAN EBERT, Psychotherapist and author of *Traditions* and *Marriages*

"*To Break or Bounce* is everything the title suggests and tons more. Dr. Shelley Plumb takes us through a powerful journey of challenges, facing the dilemmas of life—personal and professional—and making the lessons learned from the tribulations into a toolkit of resilience, success, and growth. This isn't just Shelley's story. It is a powerhouse of clarity, determination, and passion that can turn tribulations into triumph by believing in one's journey. You'll cry, you'll giggle, and you'll cry again because of the inner strength you'll recognize that is within you. Entrepreneurs, coaches, and women from all walks of life can gain so much from the brave and powerful account of Shelley's journey. Highly recommend it!"

—**SZEBASTIAN ONNE G. S.,** The 'Almost Naked CEO',
Szebastian.com Group

"Shelley's book, *To Break or Bounce,* is poignant, riveting, superbly written. It draws you into her world immediately from the very first sentence with such simple yet profound lessons that you can recognize and incorporate in your own everyday life."

—**ALICIA COURI,** Founder of Red Carpet, CEO and founder
Alicia Couri INC., CoFounder and Executive Producer, DreamaniacTV

"The raw emotion that Shelley invokes with these personal stories is both profound and thought provoking. Life throws many challenges at us, and how we respond determines the quality of the life we will experience. In this excellent book, Dr. Shelley shows us how to rebound and make the best of things. Bravo!"

—**KEEP IT FAST, GORDON,** International Business Speaker,
Executive Coach, and Consultant, Gordon Tredgold LLC

"Shelley Plumb's journey to connect with her authentic self is rich with discoveries. Along the way she courageously shares her intense struggles and inspiring triumphs. There are powerful lessons here for all of us!"

—**ELLA MAGERS,** MSW, Founder and CEO of Sexy Fit Vegan®

TO
BREAK
OR
BOUNCE

Finding Balance, Stability,
and Resilience in Our Lives

TO BREAK OR BOUNCE

DR. SHELLEY PLUMB

GREENLEAF
BOOK GROUP PRESS

This book is intended as a reference volume only. It is sold with the understanding that the publisher and author are not engaged in rendering any professional services. The information given here is designed to help you make informed decisions. If you suspect that you have a problem that might require professional treatment or advice, you should seek competent help.

Published by Greenleaf Book Group Press
Austin, Texas
www.gbgpress.com

Distributed by Greenleaf Book Group

For ordering information or special discounts for bulk purchases, please contact Greenleaf Book Group at PO Box 91869, Austin, TX 78709, 512.891.6100.

Design and composition by Greenleaf Book Group
Cover design by Greenleaf Book Group
Cover photography by Teri Roberts Photography

Publisher's Cataloging-in-Publication data is available.

Print ISBN: 978-1-62634-689-5

eBook ISBN: 978-1-62634-690-1

Part of the Tree Neutral® program, which offsets the number of trees consumed in the production and printing of this book by taking proactive steps, such as planting trees in direct proportion to the number of trees used: www.treeneutral.com

TreeNeutral®

Printed in the United States of America on acid-free paper

19 20 21 22 23 24   10 9 8 7 6 5 4 3 2 1

First Edition

To all the adventurous, beautiful, passionate souls
searching for love, light, and peace.
It is out there, my friends.
In many cases, right under our noses.

Contents

Foreword

From the first moment I met Shelley, I was struck by her high-octane energy, her focus, and the very high standards she quite clearly sets for herself. I was also touched by her great personal warmth and generosity of spirit. We met in the middle of the African bush where she was filming wild animals from the back of an open vehicle. Her relish for the adventures that met us on our travels was infectious.

What I didn't know about was any of the events that had shaped her life and, more importantly, how she had responded to them. *To Break or Bounce* is a deeply personal account, beginning with Shelley's loss of her mother as a young child. She is unflinching in describing the painful challenges she has had to negotiate—from professional burnout, divorce, sexual harassment, and losing the beloved grandmother to whom she never had the chance to say goodbye.

It is exactly these experiences, however, that make Shelley who she is today. Through suffering, she has attained insights, and these are the jewels she so generously shares in her book: the importance of embracing how things are, rather than how we wish them to be; letting go of constant striving for perfection; being flexible when faced with adversity; and always striving for balance. Shelley offers some potent images to illuminate these insights, one of the most powerful being a ball—her chosen symbol of resilience.

As Shelley so vividly shows, even in our darkest moments, when we may feel we have lost all control of everything around us, we still have the freedom to choose our response. It is Shelley's gift to us all that she is the authentic embodiment of the choice she has taken: not to break, but to bounce back from adversity and light up the world. May this book carry her light to the hearts and minds of many readers around the world!

David Michie
International best-selling author,
keynote speaker, corporate trainer, and
mindfulness and meditation coach
Perth, Australia
May 2019

Part One

BREAK OR BOUNCE

"Nothing ever goes away until it teaches us
what we need to know."

—Pema Chödrön

I Was Not There

Freedom!

Freedom is all I want as I attempt to wrestle my arm from behind my back; my brother, arch-nemesis Number One, has it pinned there skillfully. We giggle as our family's Volkswagen Bug hums along, and we pause only long enough to take in the canopy of fir trees that line the sides of the road. Their branches extend over the highway like a lush, green awning. We're in the back seat of the car humming cheerfully to the song on the radio . . . Don McLean singing bye-bye to Miss American Pie . . .

I loved that song! The Chevy and the levee . . . the melody fills my heart with fondness and cheer. We come out from under the canopy of trees and continue on our way. As if to remind us of the beauty of day, the sun streams through the window, bathing me in its brilliant warmth. I look up and take in the depths of the blue sky above. There are no clouds, and I sense a magnificent presence. Suddenly, out of nowhere, a hawk glides overhead. Her three-foot wingspan makes me gasp in awe, and she is so close to the ground that I can see her red tail feathers as she passes. I am mesmerized as she gracefully negotiates the wind. Her body in stark contrast to the blue sky overhead makes her elegance even more evident.

"POOF!"

My brother's stuffed animal smacks me upside the head. We banter back and forth, giggling, and I raise my hands up to hit him with my Mrs. Beasley doll. He's jabbing me playfully in the rib, when I drop my arms suddenly.

Something is wrong—terribly wrong.

I'm looking up at the sky. The hawk has disappeared, and the sun's brilliance has disappeared into an eerie glow behind a wall of clouds. *What is that feeling in the pit of my stomach?* I look at my mother, who is speaking with a friend in the front seat. Her beautiful features are crystal clear to me: her dark brown hair and soft skin. I notice her chic, colorful, fuchsia-and-green floral scarf wrapped gracefully around her neck. I see straight ahead out the front window as the car rolls to a stop at a faded red stop sign. We stop and then go again. The rest is in slow motion.

The squealing of rubber.

I'm moving forward from my seat.

The screech of metal.

My head is hitting the front windshield.

Screams of terror.

Everything goes black.

• • •

I force my eyes open in a futile attempt to erase the painful memory of my mother's death those many years ago. The vision of the accident is gone, but the scars that bind my heart make it impossible to forget. My grandmother has just died, and as I start to relive the events of the past few weeks surrounding her death, I realize that those old wounds have reopened.

I am having a difficult time forgiving myself: I wasn't with my grandmother when she died. There was the phone call interrupting another afternoon I will never forget. I'd been run down, sick, and disconsolate. I was overwhelmed with responsibility, lacking balance, and treading water with my nose barely above the surface. The call was the last straw. Already feeling isolated and alone, I lost it; I went under and hit rock bottom.

• • •

Staring out the windshield on the way back from Grandma's funeral, I study the rain. It streams down the window pane like the tears on my face. I inhale the fir trees—normally a welcome, fragrant scent, but now a piercing smell that overwhelms my senses and penetrates my mind. As I descend the driveway to her house, my eyes track across the lawn to the apple tree that is infused with memories from my childhood. Once so magnificent and strong, the tree now appears dreary and wilted—and empty of meaning. Its leaves hang in defeat. I recall my father's account of Grandma's last words: how she opened her eyes, how her fingers touched his face, and how she smiled. A knot tightens painfully in my stomach. *I was not there.*

The pain spreads through my body like the motion of a thousand bees in a frenzy. My stomach spasms as I recall her warm laugh. Memory brings back visions of her magnificent fried chicken, the warm fire in her fireplace, and the games of cribbage at the kitchen table in the early morning hours. She was my foundation, and in the absence of my mother, she provided much-needed balance, comfort, and encouragement through my early childhood years. My one true regret is that I wasn't there for her toward the end of her life like she was for me at the beginning of mine. It is a regret I will have to live with for the rest of my life. I stare out over the grounds of her spectacular property, taking in the apple tree, the bay, and her beautiful garden. Losing her has thrown my mind into a state of confusion, and an endless barrage of questions remains unanswered, unanswerable. The unceasing flurry of activity in my mind compounds my isolation.

How . . . Why . . . What . . . ?

> How many of us feel lost? Why do we fall apart? What holds us together? Despair is a feeling with which I thought I had become familiar, since I have seen many of my family and friends lose loved ones in the past. But it is so much different when you experience it personally. When you lose a loved one, you have to deal with a complex array of emotions. Each individual is impacted differently, but pain seems to be the common denominator.

As the car rolls to a stop and my feet step onto the gravel, a sea of despair washes over my mind. Pain comes in many forms, and it often masquerades as guilt—*I wasn't by her side,* or despair—*I'll never hold her hand again*, or loss—*I didn't get to say that I loved her one last time.*

Will this pain end? Confusion and panic mount in my head like a volcano ready to erupt, threatening to crack the outer hull of my existence. As I venture toward the garden, I feel any courage I have turning to fear, any confidence turning to apprehension, and any love turning to self-loathing and overwhelming guilt.

I know these feelings won't end until I have come to peace with them. But how? How will I ever bounce back from *this*?

The Apple Tree: Balance

My gaze comes to rest once again on the apple tree. I recall climbing it as a child, feeling comfort and safety in its lush, beautiful branches. It was a symbol of strength and security. I always felt welcomed as I climbed to the top, with its leaves serving as camouflage in early morning games of hide-and-seek with my brother. I am realizing now that the tree served as a symbol of balance in my life as a child and represented a concept I carried forward into my early adult years. My grandmother and I would talk under its canopy of comfort. Her kind facial expressions are clear and crisp in my mind against the backdrop of the lush, beautiful branches. I'm thinking of conversations with her under that tree, many of which occurred on my summer breaks from school when my brother and I stayed with her for weeks on end. During those times, I would hang on her every word, taking in each syllable with eager ears.

That vision of her triggers the memory of our last heart-to-heart conversation. I was in college at the time, far from home and working sixty-hour weeks. I had no time for family, friends—or even myself. There was no time to slow down. Let me rephrase that: *I did not make the time to slow down.*

Carving out personal time was not in my agenda. I was driven by a force few of us understand and even fewer of us question, a calamitous force that serves no purpose but to upset the grand balance of being. It is a force with real power, fueled by underlying insecurity, confusion, and fear. In reflection, I see that fear is what persuaded me

"Success comes not from reacting but from reflecting."

to keep going, no matter the cost. I was afraid that if I stopped, I would be forced to confront the inner demons that chased me through my dreams at night.

That day long ago, under the apple tree, she gave me a warning, a gentle nudge. Her words echo in my ears:

"Constantly being on the go weakens your mind, body, and spirit. Success comes not from reacting but from reflecting. You must take care of you, and you must take time to understand and heal the wounds you've suffered. Otherwise, when trauma comes into your life, you won't be able to bounce back. You'll break."

I remember her words that day, but at the time, the constant activity in my own head made her caring words impossible to absorb. As the following months turned into years, I didn't heed her warning. I kept doing too much, adding obligation after obligation. I was, in a word, incapable of saying no. My body kept going, but my mind was paralyzed by the fear of inactivity. Incessant activity occupied my mind with mundane, menial tasks so I could avoid the turmoil in my heart. Little did I know that a preoccupied mind equates with a dying spirit. I was always in a rush, and I had stopped making time for what mattered most in my life. Lost friends, severed family ties—was it really worth it?

My grandmother was always quiet and reserved. Although her small frame made little sound, her hazel eyes sang a far different tune. As a child, I always sensed a profound wisdom behind her inquisitive gaze. Was she holding something back? Maybe. Perhaps she knew I wasn't ready for what she had to say. Looking back, I feel she may have had so much more to say than she actually did.

She only let the world see subtle evidence of the undeniable flexibility and wisdom she possessed after experiencing life's turmoils and triumphs. Without saying a word, through her mannerisms and other understated hints, she preached balance and stability. Like the luminous apple tree before me, she added a degree of balance and security to my life that I have yet to find elsewhere. And her profound understanding was on display in the swiftness with which she dealt with others. She would often sit, reserved, at the table listening to others speak—only to burst into action. With her finger in the air, she would look up defiantly and say, "Don't you tell *me* what to think!"

She knew what she wanted, and she protected her beliefs. She was honest with herself and the world. She summoned strength from the quiet moments she incorporated into her life. When I was a child, on multiple occasions I saw her become agitated by an unpredictable, unjust world—ethical dilemmas in politics, bullies in the workplace, a dishonest bag boy at the supermarket. With every act that threatened her moral code, I could feel her frustration. With each instance, I would watch. Without fail, after every occurrence, she would breathe in deeply and walk outside under the apple tree. She drew strength from nature, specifically from that tree, which somehow restored balance to her world.

It's a concept I am just realizing the importance of today. Those moments of breathing in gave her time to reflect and heal, and they served as a solid foundation should a wind try to rip through life's branches, upsetting the balance. As I observe the rotten apples at the foot of the tree, the truth is all too clear: balance in life is a necessity. But back then, I didn't listen to her words of advice. I was indifferent.

> How many of us right here, right now, don't listen? We need to put down what we are doing at this very moment and really think about it. Think about those close to us, those who have struck a heartfelt chord in our hearts or even upset us in some manner. Look hard. Is there something they were trying to tell us?

I wish I had listened . . . instead I ignored the inevitable. I thought I was resilient, impermeable, and infallible. After all, the harder we work, the more successful we are, right? I thought I knew it all, and I thought I knew best. Needless to say, I ignored my grandmother's advice. In retrospect, I don't think it was success I was after back then. It was something deeper. And here I am, under this apple tree right now, wondering if the imbalance in my life has passed the point of no return.

The Bay: Control

I let the memories flow as my gaze shifts from the apple tree to the fir trees lining the banks of the bay. They provide protection from erosion and maintain the bay's beauty with unquestionable stability. Stability is something I don't feel I have right now. The personal foundation I worked so hard to build is now unstable. I stand alone on a foundation that is shaky at best. In my midtwenties, I was strong, smart, and determined—perhaps a dangerous combination when paired with naiveté.

Looking out over the waves of the bay, my eyes rest on the cool gray water that appears to go on for miles. What happens when we get to the end of a horizon that has no next day? When we arrive at our goals, do we lose control of our destiny altogether? Such thoughts haunt me. The wind kicks up, and I feel goosebumps on my arms. I feel alone. Isolated by self-defeating thoughts, I feel helpless, without an ounce of control. If I were to scream, would anyone hear me? I didn't realize what a vital component my grandmother was in my life—not until now, that is. We may have been separated by miles, but she was always there, an airplane ride away. Now she is not.

> **"What happens when we get to the end of a horizon that has no next day?"**

As a child, she was the only one I would let close. Her calm demeanor and loving words had a way of dissolving barriers. When life unfolds, it is not always kind: my barriers were a means of protecting myself from the terror, insecurity, and pain I experienced when my mother died. The protective shield I built in my life served as an obstacle to many, but not to her. She refused to let me isolate myself. She repeatedly walked past the barricades and into my heart, welcoming me with her warm embrace.

I scan the water, and my eye is drawn to a single sailboat elegantly negotiating the small waves. To many, the boat by itself, in the middle of an expansive body of water, might look isolated and closed off from the world. My mind, however, wrestles with an alternative observation. Watching the bow of the boat dance to the tune of the waves, a word comes to mind: *grace*. Yes, my grandmother negotiated the drama in her life with grace. I recall phrases she used throughout my childhood that were always simple, yet exhibited an element of grace:

"Life is life."
"What will be will be."
"Only you control you."

Yes . . . life *will be*. A thought ricochets through my mind: *The boat before me has no control over the waves or the direction of the wind.* The perception of grace exists only because the boat accepts the rhythm of the water and does not attempt to harness its power. We really have no control over life and what it throws our way. Perhaps that is why many of us feel as though we are in life's bull's-eye.

With my grandmother's passing, I stand alone and vulnerable. My stress is building, weakening my psyche, and setting me up to break when life's next drama presents itself. Gazing out at the expanse of the bay, I see the old wooden dock, a structure that tortured me as a child. I recall day after day of personal mind games as I would swim to the dock and attempt to pull myself up onto it. I experienced failure after failure each time I attempted to pull myself up only to have the waves suck me back into the water. I'd feel defeated, broken, and isolated. Day after summer day as a child, this went on. Then one day, I caught sight of my grandma watching from the shore. She shouted to me, with a grin on her face,

"Don't fight the waves. You can't control them, but you can work with them. When the waves push, let them push you onto the dock. Don't let them pull you back."

Her words of advice were magical. That day I did it. I waited for the gentle rhythm of the water to push me onto the dock. I wasn't fighting it; it was not controlling me. At the end of the day, I stood victorious on the top of the dock, my brother and grandmother joining me with congratulatory applause. I felt strong that day, no longer isolated; in that moment, I felt I was able to bounce back from anything.

I wonder how many of us feel defeated like this on a daily basis. When we spend our lives struggling for control over the drama we face, we may find ourselves alone, isolated, and terrified—battling a force that cannot be beaten, eventually cracking under its influence. Could it be that we were never meant to have complete control?

The Garden: Perfection

I continue to walk along my grandmother's property as the cracks deepen in my guilt-ridden psyche. I catch sight of her garden. I know it is her garden, but it's not the garden I remember from my childhood. It's sparse. The flowers are meek and beaten by the rain; the leaves are spattered with dirt. The rain has run off the leaves, forming puddles that drown any low-lying plants. The garden, untended, is wilted and lifeless. How I wish I'd appreciated it when it was vibrant and lush, perfect in its wild imperfection!

My grandmother loved this garden, and as I pause, I study a magnificent butterfly that has suddenly appeared and is delicately tending to a lone rose, a flower my grandmother dearly loved. It is shocking to see this garden, once a perfect vision of color and activity, now overrun with weeds and vines. The rose bushes, once lush and beautiful, are thin and gaunt in response to a year's neglect. I have never been good with plants. The few plants that were unlucky enough to cross the threshold of my homes have met a similar sad fate. Always assuming I could not give them *perfect* care, I would give up on preserving their lives altogether. Sad but interesting: how easy it is to halt efforts toward a goal if we believe perfection is not possible!

As I smell the roses and feel their satin petals, I am immediately transported back to my childhood days. In an instant, I am enveloped in a warm blanket of comfort and the same sense of overwhelming love and security I felt when we planted together. My grandmother was my mirror, a reflection I counted on for feedback. Every day in her presence, I'm

> **"How easy it is to halt efforts toward a goal if we believe perfection is not possible!"**

sure I radiated confusion, insecurity, and imperfection, and yet she would see confidence, security, and perfection in me. I always felt at ease and strong in her presence. I believed nothing could replace that feeling of comfort, security, and companionship. Today it is replaced by rain and this sad garden. I feel deflated and broken.

My memories of the roses are fuzzy, not like my perceptions in childhood that were sharp and clear. A butterfly circles erratically around a bud of the flower, seeming to search for a safe spot to land among its tattered petals. I recall working with my grandmother in the garden and watching her brush the raindrops off the petals with a gentle gloved hand, prune stray branches, and clear a path for the sun to move in and bathe the bush with its welcoming warm rays. The flowers would rebound with vigor. I wonder—do I have the strength to brush off life's drama and bounce back once again?

The insect-eaten spots on the leaves of the lone rose—once a symbol of perfection—tarnish its beauty and reflect my self-loathing. Year after year, as I watched her fertilize the base of the bush, Grandma would explain that the withered leaves did not reflect imperfection, but rather a natural progression of life. A rosebush that is flourishing is going to have withered leaves. I wonder—do I have the resources to nourish my deflated spirit, accept my perceived imperfections, and once again see the beauty within?

My grandmother's kind words and deliberate actions told a story, and I will remember them for a lifetime. She always insisted that I write down my memories on paper so I could have a mental record, a life's log. As a child, I largely ignored her request. But I am doing it now. The purpose is all too clear. Memories fade, but written words are ever-present.

The Ball: Resilience and Vitality

I continue my wanderings. Air rushes into my lungs as I catch sight of something with a red hue hidden deep in the confines of the weeds. Stooping to push away the vines, I uncover a ball. The rain has stopped, and I crouch in wonder, gazing at the ball, its red rubber bleached by years of torture by the sun. Like my spirit, the ball has lost most of its air; its outer hull has been cracked by years of abuse. Encircled in a tomb of weeds, the ball has been forgotten. It was played with diligently for years, then lost and abandoned. What a story it could tell . . . I could tell . . .

This ball served many vital purposes when I was a child here. It was a weapon, ricocheting off the head of my brother; it was a tool, used in open water to get this little girl to swim a bit farther; it was a play toy, used over years of fun as we played kickball in the yard.

I remember squealing with delight at the sight of the ball on our visits to Grandma's house during the holidays. It was a symbol of strength and excitement and, as such, took on a life of its own. Filled to capacity with air, it was always vibrant, fun, and mischievous, bouncing back with vigor from anything it was thrown against. Oh yes, what a story it could tell! It has been forgotten by many but most certainly remembered by me. Is its life's journey over? What a curious thought.

Once full of air and ready for playtime adventure, the ball is now flat, with no ability to bounce. I will admit that when I was young, I was naïve, headstrong, even a bit stubborn. Always pushing forward in life, not allowing the world to unfold in its natural state, has left me tired and defeated—deflated. I truly feel flat, like the ball in my hands. In my earlier years, the ball was more than a play toy; it was a symbol of strength and vitality. It represented the promise of a bright and exuberant future.

The mere sight of the ball was empowering, inspiring me to new heights physically and emotionally. Seeing it now, defeated and deflated, I am acutely aware of my own mental fortitude at this moment. I have let myself go, ignoring the cries of my body and the anguish in my mind. Now, I, too, stand here flat and defeated with no motivation to continue forward with my journey. My grandmother continually pleaded with me to take care of myself, get enough sleep, not skip meals, but her words fell on deaf ears. What can I do now to change course? I think of my grandmother, who was so vital to so many people, and wonder: What purpose can I serve in my current state?

Gazing blankly out at the vast body of water before me, I am acutely aware of the void in my heart. Keeping myself excessively busy over the years distracted me from the fact that the fuel for my spirit had become dangerously low. My grandmother's death has lifted the veil of illusion from my eyes; her passing has siphoned the last remaining fuel. I am empty now.

> **"Keeping myself excessively busy over the years distracted me from the fact that the fuel for my spirit had become dangerously low."**

The last thing I recall was the phone call and then tears. News of her death was the metaphorical pin. *Pop!* Years of anger, frustration, and loneliness escaped in a rush of volatile emotions. It was as though a piece of my personal foundation was suddenly pulled out from under me. I suddenly see how exhausted I am; physically, my body has been shutting down. I had been crawling through my days.

What I know for sure in this moment is so much different from what I thought I knew years ago. Back then I believed that a spirit could not break if it were never allowed to slow down and touch the ground. Today I am realizing that a spirit cannot bounce to exciting heights if it is deprived and depleted. Standing here, basking in memories, I see the big cozy chair on the porch where Grandma would bounce me on her knee and sing, "One, two, three . . . you're too silly for me!"

With those words I would fall back into her comforting, vibrant embrace. Right now, I feel my overtired body start to relax. My grandmother's presence in my life, even if separated by miles, provided an incredible sense of security for me. All my life I have been searching for answers she seemed to know implicitly. With regard to bouncing back from adversity, she always seemed to know what to do. Looking down, a sinking feeling fills my heart.

> **"How could I ever hope to channel her wisdom and inner strength?"**

All those answers seemed to have died with her. How could I ever hope to channel her wisdom and inner strength?

My gaze drops to the ball still in my hand. Turning the ball over and over, I wonder, *What do I choose?* Do I choose to buckle under the trauma and drama life throws at me? Break under the pressure? Or is it possible to take it all in stride and bounce back ready for the next venture?

It is an interesting concept. What causes one person when faced with adversity to break under the pressure, and what drives another to bounce right back, ready for the next adventure? Studying the ball, I question myself. *What do I choose right here, right now? Will I break, or will I bounce?*

As I consider the meaning of those words—to break or to bounce—I look up and catch sight of the apple tree once again. The wind has picked up, and it's whipping the branches of the tree into a mesmerizing dance. The movement transforms the tree, and it now appears beautiful with a massive, outstretched wingspan and gorgeous full leaves; luscious apples decorate the branches in a brilliant display. As the branches rustle under the force of the wind, I see how many of the branches are bending and bouncing back; I am engrossed in their hypnotic dance. A lone apple plummets to the ground. It soon is accompanied by dry branches falling from all angles. The dry and brittle branches are not able to resist the force of the wind, and they break in response.

Looking down at the ground, I realize something: *dead branches break*. If brittle from neglect, lack of sunshine and water, and lots of stress, a branch will break under the force of the wind. Our lives are much the same.

Neglect, lack of attention to what's happening in our lives, and constant activity can leave us brittle and unable to withstand the battle of day-to-day life. I focus on a branch swaying to the beat of the enchanting wind. If nurtured with plenty of sunshine, adequate water, and proper rest from the wind, it will be able to bend when the force is applied, and it will bounce right back to a place of strength and balance. Our lives are much the same.

If we live a life dominated by laughter, loved ones, and creative expression, we will have the fuel necessary to inflate our self-esteem and boost our lives to new levels of achievement personally and professionally.

> How many of us feel as though we are constantly pushing against life—a worthy opponent pushing back with surprising vigor? We may find our endurance quickly worn out in a life consumed with incessant activity. We soon become sick because of the inevitable neglect that ensues, neglect that leaves us weak and brittle—with no other recourse but to break with the force.

HOW DO WE REPAIR THE CRACKS?

Is it possible to bounce back again after our outer hull has been breached? Is there a point of no return where regaining a state of happiness is impossible? I have so many questions.

When was the last time I took a "time-out" in my life? As a mom, I often think of time-outs as punishments for children, a space created for them to pause and consider their actions. But a time-out seems exactly what so many of us adults need in our lives: a space we create to reflect, ponder, and truly enjoy the present moment, where we take time to nurture our spirits, expand our minds, and listen to our bodies. Time-outs would allow us to recover from the rotten apples life throws our way.

I am startled from my thoughts by the blaring wake-up call of some geese waddling up from the beach. My grandmother called them Canadian Honkers. They've come down from Canada and are demanding attention with their loud and needy screeching. I watch as many of them ascend into the sky, taking flight in flawless formation. As a child, I would often dream of flying free in the sky. Growing up, I thought I was Wonder Woman—invisible plane, lasso, body armor, and all. Yes, the whole bit. Flying proudly through the air, I was able to bounce back from just about anything—in my imagination.

But now, as I'm standing here, the news of my grandmother's death inflicts a deep cut that penetrates my armor and deepens with my every movement. Today I feel paralyzed. I am afraid to move. My legs are like blocks of stone keeping me anchored in place. And yet I know that something is going to have to give. *Where can I look for inspiration?* Perhaps the answer is right in front of me.

NATURE HAS THE ANSWERS IF WE PAY ATTENTION

Grandma was in touch with nature, and I, in turn, grew up with a deep respect and appreciation for the outdoors. Year after year, I watched her faithful dedication to her garden, her limitless compassion for the loud and needy geese, and the true appreciation for what each day on the bay brought.

Nature has a mysterious way of figuring things out. I catch sight of the butterfly again and am amused as it leaves the rosebud and flutters gracefully by my face. Distracted, my fingers fumble, I lose my grip on the weathered ball, and it drops to the ground. As I bend over to pick it up, my cell phone falls from my pocket straight into a puddle. Seeing it completely immersed, I recall an odd fact about the butterfly. One drop of water on a morpho butterfly's wings can cause imbalance and has the potential to damage the creature's wings permanently, making it incapable of living the life in flight it had always dreamed of. So the butterfly adapted to the dangerous rules set by Mother Nature: its wings are equipped with waffle ridges that repel water from the wing surface before it can do significant damage. Nature has allowed the butterfly to resist the force that could harm it.

Contemplating this thought, I fish through the murky water, find the phone, lift it to safety, and look at the screen. It blinks erratically and then goes black. Apparently my phone has not adapted. Go figure.

While I'm wiping the mud off the phone, a curious thought crosses my mind. Water is to a butterfly's wings what negativity is to the human spirit. One drop of negativity on a fragile psyche leads to imbalance, and in many cases, irreparable damage. We are *all* susceptible to this. The question is: How do we adapt? How do we adapt so that the negativity in a hurting world rolls off our wings? The answer is quite simple. *We must learn how to bounce and not break under the force of the negative mindset.*

> **"One drop of negativity on a fragile psyche leads to imbalance, and in many cases, irreparable damage."**

The sun peeks through an expansive barrier of clouds. Nature really does have a way of bouncing back, doesn't it? The soil under my feet replenishes itself daily despite the threat of erosion; the bush by my side grows new leaves undeterred by the beating of the wind; and the trees on the horizon grow to unimaginable heights in unstable, rocky soil. Nature possesses the glue to fill the void. It is, in a word, amazing. That is what my grandmother always said we were. We are all . . . *amazing!*

There are those among us who have found a way to rebound from life's drama and not break under its pressure. Those fortunate individuals have found an alternative form of heaven. They have found a way to live and not merely exist. "Existing" means living our lives in a passive state, waiting for each day to end so we can start the next with dreaded resolve. Who wants to live like this? The resilient among us reach deep within and find the strength needed to fill the void and move on. They are not afraid to take time-outs to pause and reflect. Much like nature itself, they are not afraid to adapt. We need to

> **"The resilient among us reach deep within and find the strength needed to fill the void and move on."**

learn to fill the cracks in our heart so we can do more than merely exist in a world where the flexible flourish and the rigid ultimately perish. We can turn the corner and go from a life of existence to a life of fascinating resilience. But to do this, *we must pay attention.*

Up until this pivotal moment in my life, I was not paying attention. Flipping through the pages in my memory, moment after moment, word after word, I recognize one solid fact: Grandma was paying attention. I, however, have been making mistakes, believing with weak resolve that my wave would continue to build and never come crashing down. Perhaps what she was trying to tell me over the years is that, like the waves on this beautiful bay, what goes up inevitably comes down. If life is not negotiated and properly planned, it comes down hard, taking out everything and everyone in its path.

The sun escapes fully from its cloudy confines, shining brilliantly. No, I wasn't paying attention then, but I am now. In reflection, I realize that through her words and actions, in her silent way, Grandma was telling me something, something very important. She was telling me that there are specific qualities a human being possesses that make up their character. When put into action, these traits give us the tools necessary to withstand the stresses of life and the strength needed in order to not succumb to the perils. Our resulting character determines whether we feel empty at the muddy depths of oblivion or feel full flying high in the sun and clouds.

> How many of us have been in that empty state where there is no peace to calm our spirit, no love to warm our heart, and no light to illuminate our path? What a beautiful feeling it must be to truly feel full, wanting for nothing, with peace and love—and light acting as a beacon telling us we are finally home. No more struggle, no drama, and no conflicts. *Ahh . . .* does such a place exist?

Yes, this place exists for the few fortunate, blessed individuals—individuals who have developed the traits necessary to strengthen their character. When negativity rears its ugly head, these individuals take it in stride, adjust, and keep on full steam ahead. These individuals have what it takes to bounce—not break—when it matters most in their lives.

As I stand here at the foot of this magnificent bay, Grandma's words of wisdom about balance, isolation, and perfection start me on a journey. I have hope that my memories will carry me to safety in the coming years. Today, I'm embarking on this journey through nature's metaphor—the happy memories and the sad, the obstacles and the triumphs. It will be a journey of quiet reflection. Her words regarding balance in life will force me now to take a good, hard look at my life. Looking out at the bay, the trees, and the flowers, I recognize that my grandmother also warned me against isolation. Her words about perfection come to me like whispers from nature, like the calm after a hurricane, the flowers after a flood, and the new tree buds after a fire. They are words of advice that can make us resilient. And with resilience, we are much less likely to break with adversity and far more likely to bounce back when challenged by life's follies.

GOD'S COUNTRY: IF YOU CARE FOR IT, IT WILL CARE FOR YOU

Grandma called the scene that lies before me today "God's Country." What did she mean by that? Quite simply, if you care for it, it will care for you. That advice applies to many things in life, doesn't it? It applies to family, friends, circumstances, and life. Everything we need to know lies in nature. We just have to open our eyes.

I'm consumed by sorrow on this solemn afternoon, but I also realize that all is not lost. I have a choice. We *all* have a choice. When pinned down by the weight of life's drama, will we break under its enormous weight, or will we shrug it off with determination and bounce back with conviction? Each of us has that choice. Today, let's all take a journey through nature's garden, a journey that will test how well we really know ourselves.

Holding the cracked, weathered ball in my hands today, I study it. Like our lives, it may be cracked, but it is certainly not broken. Intuition tells me that the pain from the loss of someone so dear to me will not lessen until it has taught me what I need to know. Let's all take a walk and reflect on my grandma's words. Let's let them sink into the depths of our soul. Let's pause. In the past I was quick to brush off her advice, but I am listening now.

Let's bounce back together.

> "Intuition tells me that the pain from the loss of someone so dear to me will not lessen until it has taught me what I need to know."

Part Two

HOUSE ON ROCK

"Life is not easy for any of us. But what of that? We must have perseverance and above all confidence in ourselves. We must believe that we are gifted for something and that this thing must be attained."

—Marie Curie

Pride and a Strong Foundation

I feel battered and beaten. Looking out over the beautiful bayside property, I see children playing happily in the distance. I had so much fun growing up here. My mind is full of vivid, exciting childhood memories. I can visualize my little brother running furiously down the rocky path in a futile attempt to defeat my six-foot-two-inch grandfather in a foot race. Such fun . . . so many memories . . . past memories.

In a haphazard attempt to lift my mood, I look skyward. Three large blackbirds are chattering angrily on the uppermost branch of the apple tree. I feel a knot tighten in my stomach. It is a feeling I know all too well. Arguing, bickering, and conflict, even if it is part of human nature, has always made me anxious. I know from past experience that if I leave it unchecked, that anxiety will escalate into something that has proven to shake me to the core: *stress*. Grandma always seemed quiet and reserved, yet beneath that calm exterior, I sensed immense strength and courage. I never questioned her inner resolve, perceiving it as strong and unshakable and able to withstand what drama life had to offer.

Her strength is a stark contrast to how I feel at this moment. My legs feel weak as I stand on a rocky foundation that is less than solid. Catering to overloaded schedules, giving in to excessive demands, and succumbing to endless activity has left me anxious. That stress, bottled up for years, has transformed me into a servant of my environment—an environment where my needs and desires go virtually unnoticed, an environment where my spiritual foundation is shaky at best. Foundation . . . oh yes, the key to surviving stress must lie in my personal foundation. To withstand the stress before me today and in the future, strengthening my personal foundation is imperative, but how?

It's curious: through the years of scraped knees and bruised feelings, I always sensed my grandmother's strength. Her stableness surrounds me, yet I feel weak and unsure. What happens now? Standing in the middle of her garden, my gaze drops again to the ball nestled in the weeds. My emotions seem reflected in the fate of the ball. The wind is blowing and rustling it from its unsteady confines. The weeds and rocks are an unstable foundation, which causes the ball to wobble back and forth—quite unlike the sturdy foundation it encountered when I was a child. I recall that it would always bounce back with vigor from any solid surface—the wall of the house, the concrete of the driveway. It bounced back instantly, its vitality never questioned. Sadly, today it is exposed, weathered, and beaten.

I savor the outdoor scents in an attempt to wipe away today's pain and replace it with pleasant memories of the past. The fresh smell of the fir trees mixed with the salt air is intoxicating, like a cocktail that transports me back years in my life. I peer over at the apple tree, so tall and stately. Its huge tree limbs extend from side to side in a perfect balancing act. It seemed at the time to stand proud.

I smile as images of my grandmother's small frame in the kitchen come to mind. As a child, I was always amazed at how quickly she could put together a hearty meal. Each meal was the perfect balancing act: the bacon done just right, the oatmeal cooked to perfection, and the fruit cut into perfect bite-size pieces. At the end of the preparation process, she would sit at the table and observe us as we enjoyed a beautiful, healthy meal. She was proud.

The concept of true pride is intriguing to me. Certainly pride is difficult to have if we are not standing on a solid foundation. How can we stand tall and reach out our arms to the heavens, celebrating a job well done, if we are not standing on a foundation strong enough to support our endeavors? I have no doubt that my grandmother's spiritual foundation was rock solid despite the hardships she endured throughout her life. I grew up staring into her kind hazel eyes, but I always knew that her eyes were not what others saw when they first looked at her. I remember the stares and snide remarks at the grocery store when we were shopping or on the beach when we were swimming.

My grandmother grew up with a disfiguring skin condition that left her with large skin lesions all over her body, including her face. Early in my childhood, I was told that my grandparents had adopted my father. I remember the emotional conversation I had with her one morning at the kitchen table after a naïve question blurted out of my mouth: "Why didn't you have children of your own?" She explained to me that she didn't want to take a chance that her biological child would have the same disfiguring condition that she had. She didn't want a child to experience the rejection and pain that she had experienced. I will never forget that day when it became painfully clear that Grandma's life had not been easy. Yet despite the struggle and hardship she undoubtedly endured, she had an inner strength, a confidence that radiated from her and bathed me in a light that always left me self-assured.

Incredible, really. Through her deliberate actions and calm words, it is entirely clear to me now that she used the adversity in her life to patch the holes in her spiritual foundation. As a child, and even into adulthood, her strength was

"She used the adversity in her life to patch the holes in her spiritual foundation."

a given, as she stood firm, confident, and proud. She taught me that true pride in oneself was not self-serving or arrogant; it was the mark of an evolved individual.

Through the years, I have celebrated success and thought of myself as being proud of my accomplishments, but was it truly pride I was feeling? Or something else? On a foundation that is unstable and forced at best, perhaps egoism masquerades as pride. We must ask ourselves, "Who is in control of our lives?" Are we? Or is it our ego? With a strong personal foundation, we have a firm understanding of *who* we are and *what* we are meant to do. Crevices and holes in our spiritual foundation can allow our spirit to slip away, leaving us insecure and unsure. When our foundation is shaky and we are unsure of ourselves, we become afraid to look within ourselves for answers. The ego latches on like a parasite and urges us to reach out to people and circumstances for validation and acknowledgment. Success that results from that process is not success. It is not real or reliable, and it is doomed to failure from the very beginning. Without a solid foundation, we find ourselves in unpredictable and dangerous situations, bouncing between fictitious success and real failure—a process that leaves us full of anxiety and overwhelming stress.

The knot tightens in my stomach again. No, today I don't feel proud; my foundation is not stable. I feel resistance building, conflict mounting, and I am not sure why. A gust of wind blows through my hair, and I start to tremble. As my mind struggles to make sense of my current situation, I sense conflict on the horizon—an internal struggle between a mind that wants to reach prematurely for the heavens and a heart that urges me to strengthen my foundation. I realize that my fear stems from internal conflict instigated by lack of inner resolve. I have felt this way before. *But when?* The fear, confusion, and uncertainty are strangely familiar to me. To the naked eye, I may have come across as strong and confident, but

> "I realize that my fear stems from internal conflict instigated by lack of inner resolve."

past experience does not always paint a pretty picture. Intuition suggests to me that there are lessons to be learned in past painful experiences.

UNSTEADY

Opening up the archives of my mind, I am transported back to a moment in time years ago.

It was one of those thunderstorm-ridden summer days Florida is known for: intense heat in the morning followed by a predictable thunderstorm in the afternoon. Flirting with fate, I run from my car to the office at the first sight of raindrops on my windshield. I arrive at the office with my hair soaked and my mascara running. I look at my watch. *Whew!* Ten minutes to spare before my first appointment. I dry off quickly and begin to prepare for the day. As my staff fills each treatment room, I put on my lab coat, pick up my pen, and proceed to treatment room number one. Sitting in the chair is a new patient, a large man, standing six foot four, who is glaring at me. His cold blue eyes cut through me like a knife. Noticing his broad shoulders and defiant body language, I am painfully aware that he could squash me like a bug. I recall hearing angry words from the waiting room minutes before. They had come from him.

"Sir, I need to inform you that your insurance is not active."

"Yes, it is."

"I am afraid your insurance company says it's not."

"Well, what do you know? Check again."

The confrontation escalates, and a concerned bystander attempts to step in:

continued

"Leave her alone. She is just doing her job."

"Oh yeah, right—and what exactly are YOU going to do about it?"

The overwhelming response to this battery of insults was stress, instant stress. It spread through the office like wildfire, affecting my staff, the other patients, and me. Normally quick to congratulate myself on being a doctor able to act efficiently in the most unusual of circumstances, I am surprised at how unsteady this patient's behavior has made me. I hadn't expected to start the day like this. The patient's cruel personal ego and his defiant steel-blue eyes took their toll on the proud demeanor I had started the day off with. The confident foundation I thought I had secured over the years was now shaky under my feet. I felt anxious and stressed. I inhaled slowly, gathering the courage to speak, desperately searching for a way to make my unsteady foundation solid once again.

As I think back to that moment from years ago, a gust of wind makes me wobble in the unstable, rocky soil. Instinctively, my hands go out to my sides in an attempt to steady myself. Support is something the magnificent apple tree never seemed to need—always perfectly balanced with branches equally distributed in a protective canopy.

A birdhouse sits on a picnic table near the apple tree, and the sight of it makes my heart sing. Though faded and weathered, it stands tall and statuesque and brings back magnificent memories. It used to hang high in this beautiful tree, while migratory birds going in and out entertained me with their sweet, hearty song. Hearty and statuesque is certainly not how I feel at this moment.

I feel emotionally unstable. I'm walking a tightrope, anticipating my demise with each potential crisis. With a heavy sigh, I think about how my personal health has been failing steadily for years, and now I stand here, unsteady on unpredictable ground, desperately trying to hold on to memories of my grandmother. The strength and confidence I remember from my childhood seem like distant memories and are of little comfort to me now. I have lost sight of who I am. Now, instead of pride, my personal ego is attacking from all angles and only serves to remind me of what I think are my own shortcomings. *What's left for me?* A state of constant stress and anxiety that threatens to suffocate my psyche and break my spirit?

> **"I have lost sight of who I am."**

Breaking versus Taking a Break

My heart and my ego are shadowboxing one another. My heart pleads with me to slow down and take some time to reflect and heal. My ego is relentless, painfully prodding, urging me to keep moving. My normal state of excessive activity has kept me distracted and conveniently focused on something other than the pain. Images of Grandma's loving words echo in my mind as I recall the endless cribbage games and how her eyes would light up in delight with each clever play of the cards. Those early morning games were my time with her—one-on-one with no one else to intrude.

I laughed and joked during our games, but on many occasions, her tone and expression would become serious. She would warn me, her hazel eyes locked on mine, about the price that we pay by meeting the demands of life with excessive activity. As a young adult, I shrugged off her tone as being overprotective and out of touch. Now I see things much differently. Back then, her tone would change from jubilant to serious when she sensed that I was overworking myself and not attending to my health because of sleepless nights, long hours at work, and excessive demands at school; she knew I was tired.

But I kept telling myself that the harder I worked, the easier life would become. When life became easier, then I would slow down. That was a mistake I am learning even today. As accomplishments piled up in my external world, my internal world became increasingly fragile. To all who knew me, I looked confident, as though I had it all.

> **"But I kept telling myself that the harder I worked, the easier life would become."**

Inside I was a scared little girl who felt she would plummet into the depths of oblivion if the whirlwind of activity ceased to exist. In the early morning conversations with my grandmother, I would chatter on about my work and studies, and she would listen intently. Her silence was commonly followed by a key phrase that echoes in my mind:

"You need to take a break."

> How many of us take well-deserved breaks in our lives? We need that mental vacation to really reflect, regroup, and revitalize; more importantly, we need to take them without guilt. Guilt is a destructive emotion often leading us down a path that is calamitous and counterproductive. A mental vacation is only a vacation if we slow down, set aside guilt, and give our mind, body, and spirit time to heal.

Grandma warned me that life is not always easy, and that the drama in life extracts the energy we all need to *live* our lives. We need that vital energy in order to express the gifts we all have. There are times in our life when it is imperative to hit the "pause" button and take the time we need to replenish our essence and express ourselves in ways that no one else can. It's the only way we can replace the self-confidence that life has stripped us of. I feel empty, and I am embarrassed about that fact. To compensate, I do the only thing I know: I go, and I go, and I go. I'm caught in a whirlwind that I am afraid to stop. Ceasing activity even for a moment is terrifying for me because I fear others will see who I truly am, and I will be forced to acknowledge what they see. I know who I am, and I am terrified to let others see this. It's difficult for me to talk about what bothers me, even though I know stress is the ultimate dictator—a monster we often feel we have little control over.

As I stand next to this magnificent tree, gazing at the birdhouse that seems sturdy and stable despite its age, a tear bursts free, and I wipe it haphazardly from my cheek. I wonder if most people believe that I am taking her passing in stride. I'm not. The emotions, pain, guilt, and sorrow are mounting inside me like a pressure cooker. The intricate balancing act in my psyche is upset. My bones ache. This, along with everything else life has piled on me, is becoming too much. It has grown—one task, one obligation, one responsibility after another—into a living, breathing entity.

THE STRESS MONSTER

When I think of stress as a monster, I picture one of my daughter's favorite childhood toys—a rubber creature with two hideous eyes and a horrifying mouth. I recall the day my daughter handed it to me with a giggle, her green eyes twinkling mischievously.

"Here, Mommy. *Squeeeeeeeeze it!*"

With a firm squeeze from the bottom, I watched in disgust as

continued

the eyes on this awful creature popped out in a grotesque display; it was horrid but strangely humorous. Through my pain today, I grin at the thought. We find the comforting blanket of humor in the craziest places. Although humbling, I realize that when I am on a personal mission, there are many similarities between me and that toy monster. There are times when I feel that I am that creature, and, if pressed too long, I'll hold my breath and my eyes will pop out too. When struck by stress, I will be the first to admit that I am a beast to be reckoned with.

We must take a good, hard look at our world. Really look at it. Stress is an epidemic.

- 43 percent of all adults suffer adverse health effects from stress.

- 75 to 90 percent of all physician office visits are for stress-related ailments and complaints.

- Stress is linked to the six leading causes of death—heart disease, cancer, lung ailments, accidents, cirrhosis of the liver, and suicide.

And the list goes on. Does stress have an effect on us? Oh yes. The statistics cannot be refuted. Stress is more than a monster; it is the ultimate villain—a villain that literally "steals" the breath out of life.

We Don't Have to Break

I'm thinking about the birdhouse perched solidly on the picnic table. *Breaking or taking a break*: there truly is a difference, is there not? We have all been at points in our life when the stress was too much and we felt as though we couldn't go on. That's often when the balance in life has been upset and excessive activity has overtaken us. It's also safe to say that there are times when our friends and family see the effects of stress within us far before we realize the extent of the impact ourselves. How many of our loved ones have taken our troubles and internalized them? When that happens, we have a vicious cycle. An epidemic. Stress breeds more stress. And when stress becomes the norm in enough individuals, we become a society on the verge of breaking. The amazing thing is that we don't have to break.

We don't have to let stress lead us down the route to self-destruction. By taking well-deserved breaks in our life, we can refill our reserves and extinguish stress before it spreads like a wildfire.

The Birdhouse: Foundation

As I ponder the possibility of breaking versus taking a break, I take a step closer to the birdhouse. I examine its foundation, its walls, and the roof of the old aviary dwelling, thinking about what a house does when we feel stress. It gives us a strong personal foundation, sturdy boundaries, and a protective barrier—all of those components in our everyday life help to protect us. Protect us from what? Life's endless drama. Obnoxious people. Obtrusive circumstances. Offensive, self-induced abuse.

With my eyes on the birdhouse, I am surprised as a gust of wind suddenly blows leaves around it in a frantic display. It seems that we spend so much time in a frenzied state that a stressful frame of mind limits our flexibility and ability to bend when life's drama pushes through like a storm on a summer's day. With one small huff, one minimal puff, our spirit comes crashing down.

I am overcome by the awesome expanse of the bay as the water becomes rough, ahead of the aggressive power of a quickly approaching storm. Movement in the distance catches my eye as a bird battles the waves. It is small, struggling, beat up by the force of the wind. As it slowly approaches shore, I notice its little legs moving furiously; but without a foot on firm ground, its forward progress is impossible. The wind, water, and the relentless current are clearly wearing the poor creature out before it can reach its goal. Constantly moving. Slow progress. Feeling tired.

> How many of us feel tired on a daily basis? Many of us are constantly on the go, incessantly pushing and forcing our way through people and circumstances. But why? What does all the activity mean? Fear . . . perhaps we are scared. Fear has an innate ability to keep us running at insane speeds in an attempt to outrun the demons that follow us through the day. One thing is clear: if we don't patch the holes in our personal foundation, the life we build will never be truly safe from the shadows in life.

The ball is still on the ground. I see the mud stuck in the cracks of its weathered rubber. It has been blown by the wind into a puddle of water, where it wobbles and spins back and forth erratically. I pause to consider a thought: the bird and the ball, the animate and inanimate, are at the mercy of the unpredictable wind. The force of the wind is offering a consistent resistance, preventing forward progress. How is this able to happen?

I realize that neither the bird nor the ball has a solid foundation, so it is easy for the wind to push them off balance in the direction it chooses.

Our lives are much the same. If we are standing on a foundation that is not solid and we are pushed by people or circumstances, we will not have the fortitude to stand firm or progress forward in our lives, and life does have a way of pushing at the most inopportune moments.

PUSHING. CONSTANTLY PUSHING.

"Pushy" is a polite way to describe the patient with the steely gaze in my medical office that day. I feel the tension mounting in my shoulders as I slowly put on my exam gloves. I am accosted by his piercing glare.

"I am not happy with you," he says. "If I am early, you should take me early."

I proceed to politely explain office policy. Surely he should understand that patients who have appointments before his scheduled visit should be tended to first. He draws in a long, exaggerated breath and expands his chest; I instantly realize that he does not or will not understand.

Recognizing that I am fighting a losing battle, I make a futile attempt to redirect the conversation to his medical condition. He launches into a detailed explanation of his ailment. I listen patiently, examine him, and begin to explain his diagnosis. I am met with an immediate interruption.

"No, no, no. You are wrong, sweetheart. That is not what is wrong with me. Here's what you are going to do. You are going to give me a shot and write a prescription for pain medicine. That is it. Got it?"

I am shocked. *Is this what I trained for?* His words sting with impact: "Hey! What are you waiting for? Let's get this over with."

My hands clench in frustration for the small bird. I watch, and my heart reaches out in sympathy. It wobbles and struggles, clearly abused by the force of the wind and water—just like the ball. As the bird gets closer to me, the brilliant green coloring on his head shows me he is a male mallard duck. I feel a wave of empathy for his plight—something the wind and waves don't have. I remember the kindness in my grandmother's words and the compassion in her body language. When the world was screaming, "Go for more," she was whispering, "Time to rest." In my college years, my workload was often unbearable. Wave after excessive wave came at me, throwing me off balance and threatening to destroy the foundation I was working so hard to build. When I lost my foothold toward a specific goal, I would beat myself up with erratic and unkind thoughts. I look back at the duck and feel my hands begin to relax.

I sense that my grandmother is with me.

I feel her hand over mine.

In times of strife, my grandmother's steady and focused demeanor would calm the waves of uncertainty in my life. I realize now that her goal was not to destroy my anxiety or wipe away my stress. No, her motives were much grander. With her kind words, calm behavior, and compassionate actions, she was able to channel my anxiety, harness its energy, and mold it into focused ambition—a personal foundation able to withstand the destructive storms in life.

As I begin to consider my personal foundation, I think: *Past pain and fear of the future have imprisoned me in a microcosm much like that poor duck's.* With my grandmother gone, I realize my world is unpredictable, and I'm somewhere that feels dark, musty, and cold, with tear-stained windows. It's eerie. I feel an air of desperation as my mind searches in sorrow for answers.

In times of stress, my instinct was always to turn within and withdraw. After all, that is a safe place for most of us, right? Or does that inward place trap us like a fly in a spider's web? We are stuck, and desperate to use our minds to "think" our way out, we overthink scenarios in life and confuse the issues until resolution or escape becomes impossible. Our minds do that, and mine is doing that right now. But when we truly look within ourselves, we see we are much more than our mind. Oh yes, we are so much more: we are our mind, our body, and our spirit—three elements have been popularized as foundations for personal empowerment. With the birdhouse as my inspiration once again, I realize that today I can put a new spin on the concept of self-preservation. That safe place we call our own can be likened to a house, can't it? Let's explore that further. If we are in our house, our safe place, the *mind* is the air permeating the space inside the house. The *body*, on the other hand, can be compared to the walls and roof that make up the structure. And the *spirit* ... oh yes ... the spirit ... so incredibly important. The way I see it, our spirit is our foundation. Without it, our safe place risks destruction and demise; it literally has no stability. When those three elements are not working together, imbalance, chaos, and stress take over.

My mallard friend is getting closer to the beach. As he nears the shoreline, I watch as one foot and then the other finds precarious footing in the black, sticky mud. He wobbles, catches his balance, and then proceeds forward slowly.

At the same time, I'm pushing at my old ball in a puddle of mud at the corner of the garden. It's stuck: no longer unsteady, but now anchored in its own prison.

The birdhouse has a piece of red yarn stuck to its old, weathered handle. I see again my grandmother's hands, and I feel my stomach tighten once more.

> I am transported back to the patient in the treatment room. I feel his eyes boring a hole through me like a dagger.
>
> He yells, "I said, that is what you will do. Do you hear me?"
>
> A surge of panic, fear, and insecurity floods my veins. I feel the walls of conflict close in on me. Time freezes. The air in the room becomes stagnant as my mind searches frantically for an appropriate answer. The assault moves to the next level.
>
> "Hey! Is anyone in there?"
>
> Priding myself on being a strong woman, I am both perplexed and ashamed of the impact this man's boorish behavior has had on me. I am not happy at all. I feel myself struggling.
>
> "Hey! I said."
>
> I find myself struggling, struggling for an ounce of strength, a thread of conviction, a glimmer of self-respect. I feel myself frozen in place.

With Grandma gone, frozen is exactly how I feel. I'm standing, staring at the birdhouse, afraid to move for fear of breaking. I feel vulnerable and fragile. If a tiny pebble blown on the wind struck me, I would shatter into pieces. Somehow, though, I must reach deep within and summon the strength, conviction, and self-respect I need to repair my tattered spirit.

Unfrozen, Unafraid: Using Stress to Create Opportunity

Stress is a silent enemy that threatens to crack apart our foundations. Stress is real, undeniable, and prevalent in all of our lives. Stress can certainly destroy—and yet we can also utilize it to create opportunity. Watching my family, friends, and myself go through traumatic situations, it often amazes me how some people handle stress with ease. They use the pressure to push themselves to new personal and professional heights. Others allow stress to defeat them and find themselves frozen and paralyzed by the fear of what *could be*. I will be the first one to admit that I have been crippled by fear on more than one occasion. Standing here now, I do feel crippled, broken. *How can I learn to use today's stress as a tool to construct opportunity?*

My mallard friend is not frozen. He is struggling frantically to free his webbed foot from its tacky confines, and as he does, I remember the words Grandma whispered softly in my ears on a stormy morning long ago when I was not more than seven years old. The bay seemed angry that day. A storm was on the way. A boy at school had pushed me off the monkey bars earlier that week, and my tiny spirit, still bruised from the incident, was struggling to understand the hate and animosity that motivated him. I was sitting on her lap, feeling defeated and hurt. She put her arms around me in a great big bear hug and turned me to face her. Her hazel eyes twinkled as she said:

"You are much stronger than you know."

At the time, her words overcame me like a tidal wave. One word comes to mind: *strength*. Her words ignited an inner resolve that I find difficult to find today. *What happened to that resilience?* I can't feel any strength right now. I feel sick when I remember her concerns for my health; she was always the first to step up and remind me to take care of *me*. What I feel right now, and what I felt in that treatment room years ago, was an overwhelming sense of fear and insecurity.

> How many of us, with each sunrise, put on that false happy face when deep down we are really sad and desolate?

I know from experience that there are consequences to behaving contrary to what we feel. Each day we paint that mock cheerful face on the sunset is a day we die a little. It's then only a matter of time before we forget who we are completely. That's a terrifying thought. The negative habits we repeat become our reality. It is only a matter of time before falsified actions become truths in our mind. When that happens, I wonder how many of us lose all sense of direction. Do we move forward or back? Like the poor little duck before me, we may wobble in the face of routine insanity.

The concept frightens me. What do we have if we focus on what others expect of us and ignore our spirit that is eager to express itself fully? In order to move forward, we must find a way to draw upon the strength my grandmother spoke of—the strength to be unafraid and give ourselves the chance to live fully. Intuition tells me that the answer lies within, in the depths of our soul. The answer sits sheltered in our "safe house," deep within, a place to be protected at all costs—a refuge that finds stability in a solid personal foundation and empowers us to feel strong and unafraid, fully capable of freeing our spirit that is stuck but not dead.

> **"Each day we paint that mock cheerful face on the sunset is a day we die a little."**

Stress affects all aspects of our safe house—the walls and the space within—and it has the full potential to destroy the vital essence of our safe place. We have all had times where stress cracked our foundations repeatedly, when there were no walls or space where we could take refuge. When there are no walls for protection and our foundation is cracked, stress has no limits and can wipe away all that is not strong and secure. I'm feeling naked and vulnerable, and then I panic at the thought of the one thing left I am terrified to lose—my memories. With my mind filled with anxiety, guilt, and shame, the soft silhouette of my grandmother's face and her beautiful hazel eyes are beginning to fade into the background. I am desperately afraid of losing my memory of her. Already I am at a point right now where I feel that everything I hold dear has vanished in an instant. I'm staring at the empty birdhouse and thinking, *This is a place I never thought that I would be.*

It's time for us to do something about the burdens society places on us and the ones we place on ourselves. We need to slow down and find a way to cope—effectively. We're not alone. I've seen plenty of friends, family, and colleagues enter into the downward personal spirals caused by stress, and I am having a difficult time with it in the present moment. I feel weary, unbalanced, and insecure. *Do I have the strength to overcome it?* As individuals in the pressure cooker of society, we have a responsibility to keep our safe house intact. In times of need, it is the only reliable place we can go to draw strength.

Let It Go

Back to my mallard friend: he is slowly making progress. With a resounding *Quack!* he frees his foot and ventures forward with determination toward a piece of bread discarded by another fellow beach dweller. Surely he's trying to get to the treasure before the other ducks spy it. I laugh and take a step back. It's just like life, isn't it? When there is motivation, we find the strength. My backward step lands on the head of a garden hoe, and as the handle shoots skyward, it upends the old ball from the puddle and shoots it to solid ground. It's on a stable, steady foundation at last. The ball comes to rest, the hoe falls back to solid ground with a thud splattering my legs with mud, and my mind continues to ponder.

"HEY! IS ANYONE IN THERE?"

"Hey! Is anyone in there?" he shouts.

I feel the splatter of saliva on my face from six feet away as this out-of-control patient takes pride in emphasizing his last word.

"Knock, knock. Is anyone *in*?"

I feel a spark ignite in the pit of my stomach. I slowly look up as my shaky smile turns to a stony gaze. Silence follows as I look him straight in the eye. I speak slowly and deliberately.

"I heard you," I say.

Clearly noticing the change in my demeanor, his voice begins to falter: "Um. That is what you are going to do. *Got it?*"

I stare back at him, plant both feet firmly on the ground, and put my pen down with a *snap*.

"No, I *don't* 'got it.' I will tell you what I do get. You are in a foul mood. You have treated my staff poorly. You are disrespectful and loud. Unless you change your troublesome, needy attitude, you can leave right NOW."

> I take a deep breath. I keep my shoulders back.
>
> "That is what I 'got.'"
>
> I promptly walk out the door and into the next patient's room.

Covered with mud and staring at the waves lapping at the shoreline, it dawns on me that one single person in the office that day was able to start a tidal wave of stress with a few simple words. I didn't ask him to come through the door like that on that particular day in my life. *He just did*. It's clear to me now that we have no control over people and circumstances—although we most certainly operate at times as though we do.

How Do We Regain Control after We Lose It?

But some stress management tool that focuses on things I have little control over is useless to me right now. What I do need is the means to control my reaction to stress. My grandmother is dead; I can't change that. What I do have control over is my reaction to that fact. How do we regain control after we lose it? How can we use stress to our advantage? I don't need overemphasized generalizations. Not everything applies to everyone. My mind is swimming with questions: *What am I feeling right now? What are the real issues surrounding my feelings? What can I do about it?*

Once again, the birdhouse offers help as I envision the precious eggs that once occupied its interior. What stresses do we as inhabitants of this earth encounter daily? Terminal illness, divorce, losing a job, debt, and chronic pain are scenarios familiar to many of us, and they have likely tied a knot in our stomachs at some point. Overloaded schedules, psychological or physical abuse, extreme loneliness, aging—the list is endless, but I stop to analyze a thought: focus is something many of us have in short supply in today's overrun, technologically dominated society.

> How many of us ignore issues that make us uncomfortable, brushing them under the rug, so to speak, and pretend they are not there? I will be the first to admit I've been guilty of that many times.

Perhaps the smart choice would be to pay attention to the issues at hand and determine whether we have control over them or not. If we do not, there's no sense in beating ourselves up. What should we do in circumstances over which we have no control? My mind struggles and then lands on three solid words: *empty the trash.*

If we don't have control over a situation, we need to give ourselves permission to get rid of it. This means letting go of self-defeating thoughts. Yes. Empty the trash. Today I am determined to clean house. I look at the birdhouse and make a promise.

I will remove the twigs—*let go of the guilt.*

I will remove the eggshells—*let go of the shame.*

I will remove the dirt—*let go of the pain.*

SOMETHING NO ONE CAN EVER TAKE AWAY

When guilt, shame, and pain invade our personal boundaries and take up residence in our safe house, devastation is the inevitable result. Ironically, many of us are terrified to remove these items because of fear of the unknown. When guilt, shame, and pain are present for too long, they become part of our identity, and when we remove them from the place we hold dear, fear may tug at our heart. What do we fear? I know:

nothing. Having nothing, being nothing, and doing nothing. It's a scary prospect for many of us to contemplate. By evicting the emotional criminals dressed as guilt, shame, and pain from our personal space, are we truly left with nothing?

Once when I was a child, I carved my initials on the birdhouse. The initials *SDP* remind me of my presence in this spot years ago. Under the tree, I pick up a lone feather, and I'm surprised how it bends between my fingers. But it does not break. Pride fills my heart. We *are* left with something. Something we all have and something no one can ever take away. We are left with our spirit. Our spirit is our foundation. I define our spirit—yours and mine—as the principle of conscious life; the vital principle in humans animating the body or mediating between body and soul.

> **"What do we fear? I know: *nothing.* Having nothing, being nothing, and doing nothing."**

I love those words—*mediating between the body and soul.* We all know that stress is inevitable. We all have stress in our lives. When a traumatic situation hits us like a terrifying storm, disintegrating our walls and threatening everything we hold dear, what keeps us from crumbling under the pressure?

SAND OR STONE?

What is left of a house that has no walls, roof, or belongings? Its foundation. I think back to Grandma's words: "You are much stronger than you know." Our spirit is our foundation. Right here, right now, in the wake of her death, I have two important questions to ask. *Is our emotional safe house built on a foundation of sand or stone? Is our spirit compromised, or is it strong?* The answers to these questions are overwhelmingly important, as they will determine our resilience and how we weather the storm.

If our foundation is made of sand, our house—who we are—will be built with difficulty. If it is built on a sandy foundation, the structure will be shaky and susceptible to destruction when the storms of stress blow through. But if our foundation is solid, we can build a sturdy mental fortress able to withstand significant force. Even if the forces are great, we can always rebuild on a foundation that has not faltered. We can rebuild bigger and better than ever before. Stress may have a temporary effect, but all is not lost if our foundations and spirits are resilient.

Oh dear God, please lend me strength in spirit.

I know my foundation is shaky at best, but my gut tells me that it is never too late to start. I wonder how many of us are committed to developing strength in spirit. It is not enough to want it. We have to believe. We can't simply want our foundation to be strong; we have to believe that it already is and spend the rest of our lives nurturing and developing it. Wanting versus believing—another interesting concept.

When our foundation is shaky and built on sand, stress most definitely can be a profoundly destructive force. If our spirit is not fully realized, if we lack confidence or self-esteem or if we doubt ourselves, our footing will not be sure. We will not have what it takes to weather the storm. There is a good chance that our personal safe house will crumble. The structure we have worked so hard to build through our lifetime will be vulnerable, naked, and destined for failure from the very beginning. After a dramatic storm, it may seem as if we have no one to depend on; we have nowhere to turn; we are nothing but failures.

No one, nowhere, and nothing. I bet that we all share a common bond with regard to this; we have all been *there*. I could talk at length about all the times when I was frozen with fear. Now that my grandmother has passed, I'm feeling the same way again. I feel frozen, fearful, insecure, and uncertain.

But remember, when stress hits us like a hurricane and destroys our walls, the space we call ours and what we hold dear, things may look hopeless. But they are *not*. We have something, something vitally important. We have what is at our core. We have ourselves.

YOU HAVE YOU. I HAVE ME. WE HAVE EACH OTHER.

I glance at the ball on the grass, and it's all clear. Until now, the ball wasn't on a solid foundation. Floating atop the puddle, it was susceptible to the wind, and like many of us, it didn't have a choice of which way to go. If our mental framework is built on a less-than-solid foundation, if our spirit is weakened even for a moment, we, too, are susceptible to being blown in the direction that other people and circumstances dictate. Our spirit is our personal foundation, and when left in its natural state, it is good, genuine, and the true meaning of self.

The strength to rebuild our lives in the way we want them to be resides within us. I get chills thinking about it. *We all have the strength, the resilience, and the confidence.* But again—we can't merely want it. We have to *believe*. We have to believe that our foundation is not made of sand; it is made of stone. With that comes strength—strength in spirit. We must unearth the skills necessary to turn stress into a tool that can be used to strengthen our personal foundation. With an unshakable infrastructure, our mental framework, our safe house, sits on something so solid, so stable, that nothing can take it down.

Intuition tells me that this does not happen overnight. Standing at the foot of this magnificent bay, my mind works diligently: the ball, the bird, the patient, and my situation right now. What lessons can I learn from them? Building a personal foundation and a mental framework that is resilient requires solid building blocks.

BUILDING BLOCK #1: READ BETWEEN THE LINES (WHERE THE HEALING IS)

Our minds are like amazing books with infinite lines outlining the story of our lives. My training has shown me that in the pressure cooker of society, most minds never stop thinking; and if they do cease activity for a moment, they often require extra help in the form of sleep aids and other pharmaceutical assistance. If that isn't enough, the pages of our novels are often dirtied by what society has spilled on them. In order to strengthen our personal foundation, we must learn to silence our minds. But how? This is a question I have struggled with for years.

My eyes move from the birdhouse to a sturdy branch above it as I recall a conversation with Dr. Susan Taylor, founder of the Center of Meditation Science in Honesdale, Pennsylvania. Meditation, I have found, means different things to different people. According to Dr. Taylor, meditation is simply "attending to the silent space between thoughts." We must train the mind to focus and move beyond the endless chatter. Only then will we embark on a journey outside of thinking and step into being. The result is a clear, calm, and focused mind where stress and anxiety no longer have a hold on day-to-day being.

As I stare at the branch, that statement has never been clearer. If our thoughts are the lines in the book of our lives, filled with row after row of chaos, then the spaces in between represent an opportunity to venture beyond and rest. The space amid the lines is where the healing takes place; it is where we plant the seeds that grow into an orchard of creative expression. It is where we connect with ourselves and reclaim who we really are.

You see, between the lines, we examine what it means to be mindful, to be present, and to fully experience life in the here and now. In this space, the past and the future do not exist. All that is important lies before us right *now*.

With my grandmother's passing, I find myself rigid, unable to bounce with the drama thrown my way. Right now, the tension is mounting in my shoulders and neck. I take a deep breath to relax, and I recall a time when a wise friend brought me through an exercise in mindfulness. I recall her words vividly. She said:

> *Close your eyes.*
> *Our focus today is on relaxing your body.*
> *Start at the top. Visualize your head and neck relaxing, your arms, abdomen, legs, and toes.*
> *Notice all the details in your current space. Focus on the sounds, the smells, the temperature, and the sensation of what is touching your body.*
> *If your mind pulls you away into drama, gently pull it back. Remind yourself you are here N-O-W. The past and the future have no power.*
> *Imagine a quiet scene that makes you feel at peace, loved, and secure. A place where loud, needy people and circumstances cannot find you.*
> *Take time to explore your space. All the senses . . . sights, sounds, taste, and touch.*
> *Take three deep breaths . . . one . . . two . . . three.*
> *Now open your eyes.*

It's amazing. I always feel a sense of calm after this exercise. I feel resilient, fully capable of bending with life's drama, and able to creatively find a solution when trauma knocks on the door of my safe house.

A Special Place to Go between Thoughts

There's the ball, sitting safely in the grass. I'm reflecting on the vision I see when I venture between the lines. It's different for everyone, I'm sure. For me, when I close my eyes, the journey takes me through a beautiful meadow filled with brilliant yellow lilies. My path then leads me through a canopy of trees that sway to the tune of a light breeze overhead. As I make my way through the protective umbrella of trees, I encounter a waterfall. The waterfall is glorious, the sun always peeking from over the top, making the cascading water shimmer brilliantly. The sweet smell of the lily tempts my senses . . . I step into the cool water and immerse my body fully. Rising back up, I taste the fresh, pure water as it trickles down my cheek. I float on my back and move freely as the water cradles me protectively. A sense of overwhelming security envelops me. After a period of relaxation, my feet find firm ground, and I slowly emerge from the water. As I walk past the tree canopy into the meadow, I feel the reassuring breeze at my back encouraging me to reenter the world—strong and confident and ready to fulfill the destiny that is meant for me.

Ah . . . that is my place, the place I visit frequently. We all have our special places, don't we? As the tree branch before me begins its own dance, I realize that I must make time and visit this place regularly. It is the space between thoughts, a magnificent place that is different for all of us. Just as we all have unique gifts in life, we have unique places to visit when we are in that space. It is our own piece of heaven designed by God to help us recoup, revitalize, and invigorate. It is where we can truly connect with our soul and our foundation when the world does its best to break us apart like the pieces of a jigsaw puzzle.

And yes, reading between the lines is vitally important in building a foundation that lasts a lifetime. It is where we strengthen who we are and silence life's chatter. The lines in life can be chaotic. If we insist on continually reading line after line, we may find ourselves broken and beaten. It is all too clear to me today that venturing between the lines to a place to recoup and heal is not a formality; it is not a luxury. It is, quite frankly, a necessity. I vow to take time daily to find a quiet place, close my eyes, reflect, and slip in between the lines.

BUILDING BLOCK #2:
LET THE NOTES BE WITH YOU

The singing of mockingbirds beckons me with a soothing melody. I listen for a moment and feel a sense of calm come over me. Images flood my mind as I realize that I grew up listening to this soothing ensemble. I recall my young eyes opening slowly in the morning to this same inviting song, coaxing me to come out to play and enjoy the day. These beautiful notes allow my tense shoulders to relax.

This sound, sweet and crisp, has a calming effect on me. It is grounding and drawing me away from my troubles to a place far removed, a place where creative adventure and prosperous journeys are paramount. Although the melodies that motivate us may be different for different people, many studies suggest that sound can significantly decrease stress. We've all had stressful days when a good upbeat song took our mind off our worries and energized us for what was to come.

Abruptly, the sweet birdsong is cancelled out by an annoying "Caaw! Caaw! Caaw!" of some black crows in a distant cherry tree. They are consuming the sweet fruit at an alarming rate, leaving none

continued

for human consumption. I find their behavior annoying and typical, as I recall many years of having no cherries as a child. The piercing cry of the crows makes the tension return to my neck. After what seems like a decade, the crows stop their nonsense cries, and I realize that throughout my life, I have taken solace in soothing sounds. The sounds of nature, music, and Grandma's comforting voice over the years have been the instruments that calmed my fears in times of turmoil. The perfect melody can be wielded like a wand to bring us calm, enhance our focus, and increase our productivity. I know this is true. I have experienced it.

FIGHT SONGS

Case in point is "Fight Song," a song by artist Rachel Platten. Every time I hear the melody, the notes strike a chord in my heart and remind me of the gifts we are given as occupants of the world. The song was introduced to me when I was dangerously close to giving up on a pursuit that I later came to know was my life's work. I recall one pivotal night when I woke in terror, thinking, *What if I fail? What if I am not good enough? What if the naysayers are right? OMG—what am I doing?*

It was a frightening experience. After lying in bed for what seemed like hours, I finally rose and went into my office. I sat in a lounge chair and cried. Sobbed is a better description of my emotional breakdown. After an eternity, I was exhausted, defeated, and scared. To take my mind off things, I grabbed my cell phone and scrolled through the downloaded songs in my MP3 player. Earlier that day, my daughter had downloaded a song she loved, and scanning the list, I noticed it was called "Fight Song." That night, I played the song, hit replay, and listened again. I replayed the song until the lyrics were ingrained in my mind. These lyrics, simple notes, and a moving melody connected with me on a level that I can't explain. It changed my life forever. Why?

IT PICKED ME UP

In the first section of the lyrics, the songwriter suggests that we are like small boats on a large ocean; it's easy to feel lost and overwhelmed by what lies before us. Although we may be a small speck in an expansive body of water, movement generates waves in the universal life field— ripples that continue through the ocean, building into large waves that can't help but have an impact on all they come in contact with. Something small, seemingly invisible and potentially ignored, can have a profound effect in the long run. In a similar respect, a solitary match can serve to ignite the flame of desire in the hearts of many, resulting in an explosion of goodwill that is felt around the world. The waves and a match—our words have many similarities. A single word spoken with positive intent can be just what it takes to help a hesitant heart open, making it receptive to love, encouragement, and self-acceptance once again. It is that powerful.

I moved to the edge of the chair that night, my tiptoes on the ground, and realized that if I can get to a single person with one positive word, a heart can be forever opened. One person, one match can make an explosion heard around the world. It is true!

IT DUSTED ME OFF

The song dusted me off and made me realize that there were so many things in my life that I wished I had said—but hadn't. I wish I had told my grandmother how much I loved her, how much she meant to me, and how my life was positively impacted by her loving presence. Those words, thoughts, and feelings would not dissipate and continued to torture me with their defying presence. They remained bottled up inside my brain, a space under pressure, its contents ricocheting from side to side in a frenzy of activity, desperate to escape. All of that negative energy, along with the people, circumstances, and what-ifs, continued to rattle around in my mind like cannonballs, causing damage and wreaking havoc. All those words of mine were bottled up and ready to explode. I recall my heart's silent plea at the time: "Do you hear me this time? You are worth more." It was a simple yet incredibly liberating statement. That night, as my inner resolve strengthened, I whispered, "Oh yes . . . I hear you."

IT GAVE ME BACK MY VOICE

As the song progressed to the chorus that night, I could feel my chest relax and my throat open. Oh yes, this is my fight song. I will take back my life! Standing here with my legs solid on a firm foundation, I will prove to them all that I am all right. No! I will prove to *myself* that I am all right. My life is worth fighting for. I am powerful in my own right. Right here . . . right now . . . I will be strong. I don't care what others believe. Their opinions do not matter at this moment in time. I know who I am and what I am meant to do.

IT GAVE ME NOTES TO LIVE BY

That night I made a commitment to myself. I made a promise to take back my life, a life worth living. The notes of the song became a part of me, and they continue to remind me how strong I really am. We are all strong. We simply have to believe—even when no one else does. The song gave me notes to live by and forever changed my life. My power was ignited. The beauty in this song was immeasurable and lifted me up that night.

One thing I know for sure: we all have our fight songs—those songs that wrap us in a warm embrace and light a spark in the depth of our soul.

There have been many others since then. Each song may be different but equally inspiring. Sometimes the melody that moves me is the simple call of the birds in a tree, while other times it is a spirited jazz ensemble that motivates me to look beyond the confines of day-to-day life. What is important is that the sounds resonate within our heart. We must listen, truly listen, to the beat and the lyrics, feel the emotions, and welcome the memories they elicit. They can be incredibly inspiring for us.

Having picked the poor cherry tree clean, the crows take flight and move to a far-off tree, taking their annoying call with them. The call of the mockingbird returns. I pause to enjoy the melody, and I feel my body relax. All is not lost. Today it is the song of the mockingbird—tomorrow Michael Bublé? I feel confident now. My feet are firmly back on the ground. The sadness is still present, but I don't feel so lost. I am more secure, capable of dealing with what life has to offer me.

Together let's continue the music and the melody—it's the ultimate building block we all need for a solid personal foundation. Let the notes be with us all! I am determined to take time daily to enjoy the music of the day, to let it infiltrate my soul and strengthen my personal foundation. No matter how painful the circumstance, we have to believe there is always hope. We have to find that melody that moves us and play it loudly in times of strife. We must let its notes be the catalyst that infiltrates our psyche and bathes us with self-confidence. May we explode into a wave of positive action, the effect of which can be seen in the bright smile of others. No matter the circumstances, I know with certainty that there is a little fight left in all of us. Look out, world!

BUILDING BLOCK #3:
TAKE THE GARBAGE OUT

I look down at Grandma's shoreline and am intrigued. The friction of the waves against the rocks is creating sea foam; bubbles are forming erratically—some large, some very small. I wonder how many of us exist in life within our own metaphorical bubble? I know that in times of strife, I often feel like I am frozen in time and surrounded by an invisible barrier. That barrier, like the foam bubbles forming before me, exhibits a degree of permeability. We and we alone control what enters our personal space.

As I reflect on the week's events, I feel the sadness, sorrow, and guilt seeping through the chambers of my heart. I know that in the last few years of my life, I have let people dictate my schedule, circumstances rule my days, and insecurity overwhelm my world; my personal barrier has been left largely unattended. I let my boundaries be obliterated, allowing unimpeded access to everything and everyone regardless of intent. Standing here now, I know that I have let myself become surrounded by a terrifying amalgamation of mental garbage that has no other purpose but to demean and degrade me. I see that I sit in the middle of this bubble without barriers, the commander-in-chief watching all I value in life disintegrate before my very eyes. I can feel myself suffocating as terrifying thoughts, negative emotions, and physical ailments close in on me quickly; if I don't take out that garbage, I sense disaster on the horizon for sure.

I watch as the largest bubbles are pushed up onto the jagged rocks; some do not survive. How many of us go *pop!* in response to the jagged threats of narcissism, bullying, or passive-aggressive be-havior? How many of us try and set appropriate boundaries in life? Reflecting back on this year, I am horrified at what I permitted inside the confines of my personal bubble: negative nonsense, demanding people, and painful circumstances.

NEGATIVE NONSENSE

Negativity is like a virus that latches on and waits for the most inopportune time to cross the barrier. Day after day of antagonistic behavior from others can lead to tension that begins to replicate in our psyche. Adversarial conduct from outside sources can eventually deplete our system, resulting in disastrous health consequences. Depletion leads to further depletion, propagating a vicious infectious cycle. Soon we may feel run down, empty, and with nothing left to give.

DEMANDING PEOPLE

I'm watching the sea foam get higher and increasingly dense, covering the rocks underneath. I have always had a difficult time saying no. Even when I'm overrun with responsibility, I often take on tasks requested by others for fear of disappointing or upsetting them. This is a feeling, I am willing to bet, that many of us can relate to. The result? Our personal space becomes inundated with demanding people—some with good intentions, others not—many of whom reside too close for comfort. We soon find ourselves drowning in a sea of commitment.

PAINFUL CIRCUMSTANCES

In my mind, there are two types of circumstances: those we have control over and those we don't. As I stand watching one sea foam bubble after another escape the safety of the group and then burst on the sharp rocks below, I realize the dreadful amount of space difficult situations can take up in our personal lives. It really is a cumulative effect. Painful memories, guilt, and shame all take up residence in our personal space and ultimately become permanent fixtures that accumulate dust. Year after year, we find ourselves adding one circumstance after another, afraid to let go for fear of the unknown. The inevitable consequence is that our space becomes crowded, leaving us anxious and weary with no energy or resources to welcome new opportunities.

Negative nonsense, demanding people, and painful circumstances all take up space within our personal bubble. For many of us, our boundaries have been too permeable for far too long. The result is a negative mind-soup that penetrates our soul. One alarming consequence is that the disruptive garbage in our minds often comes out of our mouths or becomes apparent in our actions when we don't expect it to. The result is a tidal wave of stress—affecting all in its wake. Today, I tell myself, I am determined to take the garbage out, set strong boundaries, and diminish stress levels. How will I do this?

POP THE BUBBLE

The negativity bubble, that is. We need to realize that we can't possibly control every argumentative person and every negative circumstance. We do, however, have control over our reaction to the negativity directed our way. We must take the helm and learn to catch-and-flip negative situations. When we feel suffocated in a sea of adversity, we must summon the courage to acknowledge it, catch it, and flip it into a positive. For some, this may seem like an exercise in futility, but I assure you it is not. By acknowledging negativity, we become aware.

I am no stranger to negative thoughts. I recall working as an extern in a prestigious program while in medical school. I was excited to work alongside one of the most brilliant minds in foot and ankle surgery, and my attending physician seemed thrilled with my work and took extra time discussing the latest topics with me. One night, he invited me to dinner to discuss working in his program. When I arrived, I was dismayed to find that he had invited me to a bar, where it became clearly evident that he was not interested in discussing my career. My skin crawls to this day thinking about it. I can still feel his hand on my shoulder and his breath on my neck as he stepped close to me.

He made it quite clear that night that my career would do much better if I would bend to his will. I declined. I left, and it was clear I would not be invited back. Driving back to my dormitory that night, my mind was filled with frantic thoughts. Those thoughts quickly catapulted me into a dark state marked by fear, resentment, and outright hate. In my eyes, my professional career was damaged. All I had worked so hard for was now out of reach.

The next morning I woke up and looked at the mascara-smeared image that stared back at me in the mirror. *How DARE he?* I thought. *I have worked so hard and have come so far. I will not give in to this abusive behavior. I have a choice. I can let the negative cloud in my mind keep me from what I am capable of, or I can catch those thoughts and turn them into productive energy—excitement for who I am and what I stand for.* The realization that morning lit the path for my career going forward.

It became clear to me that when negative thoughts are caught and put into proper perspective, an energy is generated that illuminates our world. That light shines bright, illuminating the darkness, allowing us to see a situation for what it really is. With a clear view, we are able to catch the full meaning of the negative thought or action, fully appreciate the intent behind it, and make productive progress toward an amicable resolution. In some cases, a happy ending comes from dealing with a situation head-on; in others, a positive outcome means merely walking away from the situation entirely. The beauty is that the choice is ours.

SERVE THE EVICTION NOTICE

We cannot feel bad about evicting demanding people from our personal space. No matter how much they whine, how much they cry, and how much they scream, demanding people must stay outside the boundary and can only enter if they behave. We have a right to live comfortably in our personal space. It is as simple as that. To be blunt, we set our boundaries, and we are the ones in control of who is invited in and who is not.

That lesson became clear to me with a close friend of mine. The circumstances in her life had left her homeless. My husband and I took her under our wing, opening our home and hearts. We offered a shoulder to lean on and suggestions to consider. She met each suggestion with negativity and passive-aggressive behavior. When that behavior started to be internalized by my family and slowly began tearing our family apart, we had to act. We had discussions with her, but ultimately we had to put distance between us. After that experience, it became clear to me that boundaries in life are essential. There are times when we must stand firm and make it clear to all that narcissism, endless complaining, and demanding behavior will not be tolerated.

STRENGTHEN THE BARRIER

One of the roles bestowed on us at birth is that of border patrol guard. Recalling my little girl slapping a toy out of a small boy's hand at preschool, declaring with a growl, "Mine," it is clear to me that we inherently know as children how to patrol our own personal boundaries. We intuitively know what should be allowed through the barrier and what shouldn't.

When we grow up, though, things often change. Physical challenges and emotional trauma from a lifetime of experiences put holes in the protective layer. Without hesitation, the good and the bad get in, infiltrate our space, and suffocate us in the process. It's crucial to know when it's time to repair the barrier. Painful circumstances that we have control over must be let in and dealt with promptly. It's the only way to resolve them. Procrastination is not an option and will only serve to compound our fear. It's essential we keep the circumstances we cannot control outside the bubble so we don't internalize them.

That lesson became all too clear for me when I was growing my business. Early on, my personal barrier was highly permeable, and I allowed all opinions, both positive and negative, to influence my decisions. I explicitly remember the day I told a colleague about an idea I had for a new business venture. I explained the details, and as our eyes locked, I was shocked at what I saw. His face was cold and expressionless. "You will fail," he said.

After that hurtful conversation, I was overrun by "what-ifs," worry, stress, and fear. Finally, exhausted and sick, I sat down one day and evaluated the situation. On a sheet of paper, I listed everything I was worried about. Ironically, 95 percent of my worry was over things over which I had absolutely no control. My rational mind screamed, "Then why are you worried about them?" That day I sat down to repair my personal barrier, and to this day, I work hard to keep those circumstances over which I have no control outside where they can do little harm, even if I still remain aware of their existence.

As I take a last glance at the sea foam at the shore, I notice one resilient bubble able to withstand the effects of the hazardous rocks; it is the lone bubble that remains intact just in front of me. It only takes one, and with a smile, I realize that with effort, our personal barriers, like the bubble's, can remain intact. By promptly dealing with society's negativity nonsense, serving the appropriate eviction notices, and strengthening all the important boundaries, the third block in our foundation will be rock solid.

BUILDING BLOCK #4: BECOME A SCULPTOR

Looking up from the bubble, I catch sight of a large boulder near the steps down to the beach. Red algae line the cracks in its surface. The large rock reminds me of something—something I have seen in the past. The boulder is shaped oddly; it kind of looks like . . .

A grinning bald man—if only I could remove the seaweed draped haphazardly over the top. A bad comb-over . . .

A half-inflated soccer ball—if only the grooves in the stone were oriented in the right pattern. Maybe a basketball . . .

A huge apple dropped from a gigantic tree—if only it were less lopsided with better symmetry. Not like anything I'd ever eat . . .

Glancing up from the boulder, my mind races back through the silly scenarios, ruminating over each possibility until it is a single blur of frantic images. Crazy mind. Crazy thoughts. Thoughts that never stop, an endless loop continually analyzing people and circumstances, picking out what needs to be changed in them in an insane effort to make them what they are not. Perhaps strengthening our personal foundation has a lot to do with venturing away from this way of thinking and using our minds to mold, to sculpt. Mold what? Molding seemingly adverse events into beneficial ones. I have a curious thought: I have done this a few times in my life. How did I do it? I had to realize and recognize. It is really quite simple.

Staring at the boulder, my mind works feverishly: the lines, the edges, and the patterns in the rock. So many images are flying through my brain. Soon all the features flow together, and detail is lost in the red grooves of the granite. Right then, I remember a recommendation by a psychotherapist colleague. When your mind is stuck in an endless loop, think *red* and realize that it means STOP!

My mind freezes on a single groove in the stone. Drawing in a deep breath, I murmur, "Stop . . . stop . . . stop . . ." My brain freezes, distracted by the chant. It's a momentary and welcome pause.

Think about it. How many of us take time to stop the incessant brain activity, activity that blurs the true image of reality? We need to slow down, stop the frenzy, and take time for ourselves. Sometimes it's easier said than done. Taking time for ourselves is not selfish and is, quite frankly, a necessity, a necessity that enhances our ability to focus on the here and now. By truly focusing on what is real and important in the present moment, only then can we stop the roar of activity within that blurs our vision.

RECOGNIZE THAT CONSTANTLY SEEKING SOLUTIONS LEADS TO POLLUTION

My mind is fighting me; it is struggling to get the frenzied thought pattern back online by thinking, organizing, and analyzing. Over and over again. Our minds are always looking for a solution. A thought occurs to me as I see the cool gray surface of the boulder blend with the background. Perhaps constantly seeking solutions in life leads to pollution in our minds. I grin at the thought. I am a self-proclaimed Ms. Fix-It. If anyone has a problem—friends, family, strangers, dogs—even the helpless worms on the hot sidewalk that I have to save by putting them in the grass before they die—I immediately go into problem-solving mode. Whenever I am presented with a problem, I feel obligated to fix it. How many of us belong to this torturous tribe of tired individuals?

The thing is, there are times when things can't be fixed. We may find ourselves frantically searching for a solution that can't be found. The result is painful tension that builds in us like a pressure cooker. I think about a piece of literature by psychologist Dr. Alice Boyes, who coined

> "We may find ourselves frantically searching for a solution that can't be found."

the term *rumination mode*. She states that people often believe that overthinking will lead to problem-solving insights. But it generally doesn't. Instead, it pollutes the archives of the mind with useless riffraff. Trying to stop overthinking can be difficult, and ruminating when we're feeling down or low only impairs problem-solving. Interesting. When we stop our excessive mind activity and realize that constantly searching for solutions leads to pollution in our minds, we finally find ourselves free to see the world in its true state.

As I look at the boulder once again, this time I simply see a rock—a rock in its natural state. Yes, a rock that as an adventurous little girl I used as a spaceship to explore the galaxy, a horse to gallop through the prairie, a stage to sing my best hits from—but merely a rock nonetheless.

A comforting feeling comes over me. My adult mind realizes with crystal clarity that as a child, my mind was truly free. My mind at that time was not frantically looking for solutions, and there was no pollution to clutter my thoughts. I was free to explore real possibilities, to be creative and sculpt my world. Standing here gazing up at the blue sky, the hair stands up on my arms. Oh yes . . . the ability to create, to sculpt our world, is an essential component, a necessary building block in a solid, beautiful foundation.

I AM STRONG

It's time for me to brush away the mud splattered on my legs by the hoe. A few resistant drops stubbornly survive my haphazard attempt, and the thoughts of cleaning take me back to the sight of the duck, then the old red ball, and finally to the recollection of the patient in the treatment room. I feel an odd sensation deep in my stomach. But it's no longer the tight spasm I felt earlier. This is different. *What is it?* I wonder.

There is fire brewing in my heart. I feel it ignite something deep within me, and I suddenly face a fact: I *am* strong. *I am stronger than I give myself credit for.*

> How many of us muddle through our lives without giving credit where credit is due? When it comes to ourselves, we often brush positive attributes under the carpet, offhandedly disregarding our God-given gifts as ordinary or not worth the thought. We really need to look under that carpet . . .

The day I haphazardly brushed those attributes underneath the carpet was a day of unfortunate spring cleaning. Today I realize that if we look under the carpet, we just might find the building blocks of a rock solid foundation, one that is able to bend with the forces that are applied through the lives we live. Under the carpet we will likely find a lot of overdue credit—credit that we have not given ourselves for the things we have accomplished and the hearts we have touched in profoundly positive ways. We have to lift the carpet and not merely peek at what's underneath; instead we need to throw the carpet away. Once we do that, we can celebrate those vital elements that make us who we are.

As I brush the last of the mud off my legs, I see the ball that is now resting solidly on the grass. The wind is blowing, but its erratic antics do not disturb the ball now that it is planted on a solid foundation. *A solid foundation*—yes, that is what I have. Without knowing it, I have made use of my foundation to assist me in difficult times.

LET'S START OVER

I finish treating the next patient and notice that the door to the first treatment room is still open with the light on. I walk into the room, fully expecting the unruly patient to be gone or, worse, ready for round two. The hair stands up on my arms as I walk in and see he is still in the treatment chair. He says, with his eyes cast toward the ground, "I am sorry."

His shoulders slump in a sad gesture.

"I lost someone close to me recently. It has really hit me hard. Do you mind if we start over?"

I smile and say, "Oh yes, of course. Let's start over."

We can build a new foundation.

The key to bouncing and not breaking under the stress of life lies in acknowledging our spiritual foundation and standing firm. Those of us already with a solid foundation must realize it and explore its potential.

I'm now acknowledging that I am standing on an incredible foundation built with magnificent blocks I learned to put together myself over the years. Grandma always knew I had it in me. She helped me uncover the strength and realize my true potential. The building blocks—the ability to read between the lines, to use music to affect the soul, to take life's garbage out, and to become a creative sculptor in our lives—are engrained in our psyche; they're deep but retrievable. No one will build our lives for us. We must be the ones to do it.

Incredible. We must find the strength within. Reflecting on her words, I realize that there is firm, unshakable moxie in all of us. Oh yes, I feel it. It is there. When I reflect back to that rock bottom moment with the man in the office, there was a point when I was frozen. But I had a choice. I could let him shake my foundation, or I could stand firm, strengthened by my resolve from within. I know what I choose now: I choose right here, right now, to stand firm. I will start over if I must.

> **"No one will build our lives for us. We must be the ones to do it."**

The choice to stand firm is about commitment and faith. In standing strong we are exercising the will of the heart and showing the mind that there is nothing negative in forgiving and moving on. With a courageous presence we send a message to the universe that we can turn over a new leaf with grace and skill. We have all earned the right to navigate our lives without stress or apprehension. For some, that premise starts today. I am confident that I have most certainly earned that right. We all have earned that right.

YOU ARE STRONGER THAN YOU KNOW

You see, there comes a time in our lives when we come to a fork in the road. Off to the right is the path we are familiar with: the destination is well-known and there will be no surprises. Off to the left, on the other hand, is the less-traveled path that holds limitless, exciting possibilities. Which path do we choose? The path to the right has served us well, but it is now time to acknowledge the positive, feel the strength, and venture off to the left into new territory filled with beautiful possibilities. Focused on the ball at this moment, I realize that we must be determined to bounce, embrace the supportive feelings, confront the problems, and pair them with valid solutions. It is the least we can do in the name of self-preservation.

So, here I am. Like many of us, I have had turmoil and strife in my life. But now today, a spark has ignited. It's such a strange feeling. It's not an uncomfortable sensation; instead it is exhilarating and exciting! I feel my sorrow lessen as I realize how strong we really are as human beings. I again gaze at the lush green leaves of the apple tree. Raindrops collect on its leaves, forming small drops that slowly fall to the ground. So calm. My grandmother was just that, a calm force in my life, urging me to examine what it means to truly *live*. I miss her. I will always love her. Her words echo in my ears, "You are much stronger than you know."

She was right. Unknowingly, I have spent years putting together the building blocks of resolve from within. I am the one who made it happen. We all have that strength; we just need to open our hearts and welcome its existence.

WE ARE GIFTED FOR SOMETHING

The view of this magnificent bay and beautiful apple tree has been a welcome distraction; it has made me stop and focus my thoughts. The wind has died down now, and the water is no longer rough; its surface is smooth and reflective, much like glass. The sun's presence has been scarce up to this point, but its radiance is suggested at the rim of a passing cloud. My ball, my wonderful ball, sits contently on the grass, resting on its firm foundation and unscathed by the wind. As I stand secure, I am oddly comforted by its wise and weathered presence. I catch sight of my proud mallard friend, contently consuming his treasure, the bread he worked so hard to get.

Drawing in a deep breath, I realize that the stresses of life don't have to have such a detrimental effect on us. The balance we seek in life is achievable. We must develop the courage and the strength necessary to convert stress from a tool of destruction to a tool of construction. Life is not always easy; we know that, but with a strong personal foundation, we can persevere.

The power to do this lies within each of us as individuals. The turmoil created by day-to-day drama is ours to control. Perhaps it's time to stop trying to change the people and circumstances around us and instead focus on changing the way we react to stressful events. Looking out at the bay, the rocks, and the ball, I realize today that truly the only person I have control over is me. What we must remember is that we all possess a unique gift. That power resides within all of us and serves as the glue that seals the cracks in a personal foundation that has been challenged over time.

Is our safe house built on a foundation of sand or rock? Is it destined to be destroyed forever or to live indefinitely? By focusing on reading between the lines in the book of life, letting nature's notes touch and inspire our hearts, taking out the universal garbage, and giving ourselves permission to sculpt our future, we can build a magnificent, balanced life no storm can tear down.

Gazing at the ball, my heart softens. Yes, I can certainly speak from my standpoint: a solid personal foundation has ignited my spirit so that when fear grips my heart and stress comes knocking at the door, I will be better able to weather the storm. Today I am challenged. I will take the unstable, sandy portions of my foundation and turn them to rock; I will put those building blocks together with blood, sweat, and tears if I must. I will fill my house with positive thoughts that motivate and inspire.

We all need a special kind of inspiration that empowers us to soar to new heights. That power is ours: it's the power of choice—the choice to let go of thoughts that shake our foundation and welcome those that strengthen it. *Let's bounce back with vigor!* We will build on a solid foundation first and foremost, a foundation on rock, not sand. Wow—there is no telling what can be accomplished! The bottom line is that we will always have to deal with storms. Stress and negativity will always be present to threaten our inner sanctum. We all know that drama in life can create repercussions that shake the walls of our very being. But we are gifted for something, and when our foundation is solid, *we are unshakable.*

Part Three

ISLAND-CLOSE

"People are lonely because they build walls
instead of bridges."

—Joseph F. Newton

Will There Always Be Time to Live and Love?

A brilliant array of colors is reflecting off the water today at my grandmother's property. I take in the beautiful shades of blue, green, and a touch of fuchsia. The bay is smooth as glass until a lone raindrop pierces its dazzling surface, sending ripples of disruption across the water. I follow their progression where they disappear into the mist at the horizon. I feel an odd sense of discomfort mounting in my heart. The mist is creeping toward the sky in an eerie barricade and inching closer to me like an impenetrable wall. My mind is becoming skittish and starts to test my psyche with nagging nonsense. Why does a wall of mist bother me? I watch as it builds steadily upward, reaching for the sky. I feel it's separating me from the outside world. But honestly, I have always felt separate from the outside world; I've always felt different in more ways than I can count.

When I reflect back to my childhood days with my grandmother, I remember how she was always interested in hearing about my interaction with friends, family, and boyfriends. She listened as I spoke intently. She always smiled and laughed at the loving and humorous interactions I described, and she always offered words of encouragement if a relationship hadn't worked out as I had planned. Through her words and actions, she unfailingly taught me that healthy relationships offer a degree of complexity, but they always rest solid on a foundation of strength, stability, and trust. As the misty wall nears, I wonder, *With a barrier between two individuals, how can a productive union occur?* Terror strikes my heart as I realize that the barricade looming on the horizon promises isolation and seclusion. I suddenly feel frozen, lonely, and afraid. I am unsure.

Pushing the thought away, I come back to the colors reflecting off the water. Their brilliant display reminds me of my grandmother's inner strength, something that always comforted me, and I face the fact that the wall of mist represents the metaphorical barrier I put up between us over the years. It was a wall that prevented real communication and loving interaction on my part in my later years, in spite of all she gave to me in my childhood.

Now that she is gone, my heart yearns for something more than superficial communication. As a child, my relationship with her was solid. She was one of the few individuals I trusted. Sadly, as I matured from a child into an adult, a barrier grew between us—a sneaky, foggy barricade that developed slowly, without my awareness . . . until it was much too late to do anything about it. Oh, how I long to be close to her now! I regret letting time and distance come between us. I always felt there was time, time in the future, but now it is too late. Fixated on the mist off in the distance, my mind jumps from one thought to another.

> Why are some of us reluctant to open our heart to others? Why do we build barriers that prevent the closeness we long for? How many of us live with the notion that there will always be time to live and love?

Life's Big Peck

A gaggle of geese has congregated on the shore. They're a noisy bunch, honking excitedly as they wander up the path from the beach. Flocking together as one unit, their individual beauty amazes me, each with a long, graceful neck and black-and-white feathered wings. Gorgeous.

I stand as still as I can as the gaggle waddles up the path to the yard and comes to a halt not six feet from me. The geese seem oblivious to the fact that we are so close. Curious and confident, I step forward and outstretch a friendly hand. A lone goose turns and looks at me, stretches his long neck out defensively, and cocks his head back. He looks like a gun ready to go off. *Oh dear God, will he bite?* The question goes answered as he lets out a loud, drawn-out *H-I-S-S!*

The sting of rejection is something I have become all too familiar with over the years. From bullies picking fights in grade school to professional dismissal and sexual harassment as an adult, I have dealt with rejection on more than one level. I jump back today—immediately fearful that my actions might provoke an attack. Message received! I would like to keep my fingers today, thank you very much. Interesting that in less than a second, my confident, fearless demeanor withered away to one of apprehension and uncertainty under the heat of rejection. I violated his personal space, his invisible wall that delineates his comfort from his discomfort. How many of us put up similar walls in our lives? A barricade we stand behind so we feel comfortable, safe, and calm—a blockade that if breached by others leaves us uneasy and feeling the need to hiss and strike?

Without warning, the birds scuffle and squabble among themselves. Some are pecking; others are honking. I watch with fascination as feathers fly in a flurry of activity and a flapping of wings. The source of the altercation is a large goose standing at the center, who is clearly the aggressor in the bunch. Evidence of past battles are noticeable on his body in the form of missing feathers and healed cuts on his legs. As if on cue with my thoughts, the enormous goose juts out his neck and lets out a long, drawn-out *H-O-N-K!* It's a different sound from what I heard before. Is it a welcome call? Something else? It has gotten the attention of the surrounding geese, who are staring at him apprehensively. Just then, I notice a smaller goose move closer to the large bird. He obviously perceived the call as a welcome signal and moves closer, attempting to join the mainstream group. But that was a big mistake!

The dominant goose lowers his head slowly, bobbing it up and down. Then, as if in slow motion, he lunges forward and attacks the small, unsuspecting bird. Feathers fly in a thrashing of wings and a blur of beaks. The smaller goose puts up a good fight but quickly becomes overwhelmed and retreats to a lonely corner of the lawn. I feel sorry for him.

Contemplating the interaction between the geese today, I can't help but compare it to human life. I think many of us will agree that life has a way of inviting us in, enticing us to reach out, and then—*uh-oh*—surprise! Life's big "peck." Oh yes, this has happened to me more times than I will admit. In an instant, faith in ourselves turns to fear. I sigh as memories flood my mind: being delighted as a teenager when a boy asked me to homecoming, only to find out he did it as a bet with his friends; in college having a professor encouraging me to speak up in class, only to chastise and mock my answers; working hard as a trained professional and beaming with pride at a job well done, only to have my boss tell me I wasn't producing enough revenue. Yes, life can have a relentless "beak" that can leave us feeling bruised and battered after an attack, and we often withdraw in a lonely retraction.

When we're under this cloud of negativity, it's difficult to savor the beauty in our lives in the here and now. You see, this cloud or mist is heavy and oftentimes seemingly impenetrable. If it's not carefully monitored, it threatens to envelope us like a straitjacket, making it difficult to breathe and see clearly. We lose sight of the beauty that surrounds us, but more importantly, we lose sight of the precious gifts that lie within us.

When that happens, we may find ourselves feeling as if there is nowhere to turn—in a terrifying place, lost in the dark. Oh yes! As my mind drifts to a place in the past, I realize that standing before the bay today, I feel lost . . .

LOST IN A CROWD

That is how I felt one day at the zoo. Smelling the pungent odor of the animal tents mixed with the unappetizing smell of cotton candy, I'm surrounded by a flurry of activity and a blur of people. It's ironic, because I have never felt so all alone. Alone and confused; I have always feared that combination of emotions. I look down at my youngest son who stands beside me, looking up with crystal-blue eyes, the curls of his red hair sticking up on the top of his head and chocolate visible on the corner of his mouth. He is excited, pulling on my skirt. "Come on, Mommy! Come on! The petting zoo! Let's g-o-o-o-o-!"

His voice becomes higher pitched as he pulls on my hand. I am clearly not in the moment; my son's enthusiastic banter and wide eyes go sadly unnoticed. I am distracted, disturbed by a career-threatening mistake I made months ago in hiring the wrong person for a very important job.

I let go of my son's hand and insist on resting on a nearby bench. I watch him play idly nearby. My stomach tightens involuntarily as I remember the events earlier in the day. One word keeps popping into my mind.

Why?

I had been working sixty hours a week trying to get a business

continued

endeavor off the ground, navigating strange yet invigorating territory every day. My exhaustion and frustration had reached an all-time high. Developing a new business is difficult enough without people taking advantage of your goodwill. The consultant I had hired months earlier made critical business decisions without a thought for my company or the team running it. I seriously regretted the day I decided to hire him. He certainly "talked the talk," claiming he could do the job faster than anyone, increase revenue, and double our exposure to clients—plus, his credentials and references were impeccable. I hired him with high hopes. I thought I had found a team member to depend on. Soon into the relationship, however, it was quite clear that his motives were not pure. Hopeful anticipation quickly turned to anger as deadlines passed, revenue plummeted, and projects went undone.

His narcissistic behavior had become overtly evident earlier that day as he stood before me, his nose in my face, glorifying his value and undermining our team. I will never forget his words: "You need me more than I need you [laughter]. If you let me go? Hmmm . . . perhaps I will open up a new business and compete with you. I see what you are doing wrong, and I know I could do it much better." He wielded words like a dagger, inflicting wounds that would be slow to heal. How could I have been so stupid? So trusting? So naïve? I think what hurt the most is that I thought I had found a partner—someone who cared, someone to share the successes and the failures. Staring at the pavement now, it is clear: there was no success today. Today's meeting was composed of angry emails and accusatory words, and the finale was me saying, "You are fired. We won't be needing your services any longer."

Looking at the ground at the zoo today, a few involuntary words escape my lips that I pray my son did not hear. The relationship with my colleague has clearly ended. Now I stand here in the middle of the zoo desperately attempting to shake the experience and enjoy time with my son.

"Mommy?"

I look up and find his big blue eyes gazing at me with a concerned expression.

"Can we go in now?"

My heart searches for answers. Today was the end of a business relationship, but a month ago there was turmoil in my family. Why do people say things that hurt? Why do they say one thing but mean something entirely different? It makes it difficult to know who we can trust. Do we trust until there is a reason not to, or do we take a more pessimistic position and mistrust until people show us that their motives are honorable?

My mind and heart shadowbox the ideas back and forth. My mind is entwined in the drama of today's events, even as my heart yearns to join my little boy in the petting zoo. I am intrigued as he slowly approaches a small baby goat. The animal is hesitant and runs to the corner of the pen, leery of my son's presence. It is clear she does not want to be close and is intent on keeping my son at a safe distance. My little boy shrugs his shoulders and starts feeding the momma goat, a tactic soon to be rewarded as it gets the baby's attention. I grin as the little creature bleats and prances to the center of the pen, her tail twitching back and forth, eager to see what is in his hand. My son lets out an ecstatic belly laugh as the baby goat nudges his leg with a cold wet nose and buries her face in his pants pocket. Those big blue eyes peer up at me once again, this time proud to show me his newfound friend. I watch as he begins to feed his eager playmate.

One pellet gets her attention.

continued

Two pellets make a connection.

Three pellets establish trust.

Attention. Connection. Trust. What a great combination!

My heart wins the battle, and the day's events fade away. I watch my son in the present moment walk from one corner of the pen to the next with the baby. The pellets are held out in a warm welcome, obviously accepted, as I notice the little goat chewing contently. My son looks up at me, his face beaming.

"This one likes me!"

They walk together uninhibited as if in their own little world. All walls have been obliterated; a bridge to friendship has been built with kindness and solidified with compassion. I watch as my son pets the goat and says to her, "Come on, let's play!"

I am amazed as the goat prances gleefully over to him and closes her eyes as my son scratches behind her ears. So trusting—and so fast, all barriers dissolved instantly. He has found a new buddy. Both parties are clearly in the moment, enjoying each other's presence. Is life really that easy?

Fear, Deception, and Honesty

Fear has been a significant part of my life over the years. Over time, I have kept many people at arm's length for fear of being hurt or misled. I know I'm not alone. Standing here now, gazing at the flock of geese in the lush green grass, I am acutely aware that I allowed a barrier to be built between my grandmother and me over recent years. I watched her grow older, and that scared me. Why? Because I loved her. Instead of inviting her in closer, however, I put up a barrier, a smokescreen composed of lost time, distance, and illusion, hiding what I was truly feeling underneath. I thought, *There will always be enough time, distance doesn't matter, and memories are an illusion.*

Here now on this beautiful blanket of grass, looking out over the foam-capped waves, I feel my breath catch in my throat. I always thought there would be time—time to catch up, time to reconnect, time to laugh. Recalling my tears at her funeral, I realize that I carelessly let time slip through my fingers. I let distance creep between us, breaking a connection that was rock solid when I was a child. Oh, how I long for that connection now. Through the years, I have been content with my memories of her, but they were never the same as real live moments in her presence. Memories can be illusive, lulling us into a false sense of security. I realize I allowed my memories of her to be a substitute for real interaction. What a costly mistake! The thought saddens me. Yes, time, distance, and illusion can become a barrier we are not aware of until it is too late.

An unseen barrier appeared to be flaunted today by the large goose's mock invitation to the smaller one; a nonsense signal lulled the less dominant one closer, only for it to be rejected. Many of us know the sting of rejection all too well. Oh yes, I know that feeling; when people say things to us that are destructive, condescending, and passive-aggressive, it tears through our hearts like a dagger driven deep with destructive intent. We tend to focus on what others have done to us, but I can't help but wonder, *Do we ever do the same?*

It's essential that we be honest with ourselves. When we are angry, hurt, or anxious, how easy is it to utter curt words, sneak a nasty glance, outright ignore, or observe someone with overt disdain? I will be the first to say that I have certainly acted that way at times. *In life, do we always say what we mean?* My mind soon grows tired of this dark course of thought and struggles to pull itself off that path. I look at the ground and chuckle. I don't always say what I mean—especially when I am tired, hungry, or, heaven forbid, I haven't had my coffee in the morning. Lessons of the past come front and center, and my demeanor brightens.

OH REALLY?

Although I don't always say what I mean, I have learned that others don't necessarily say what they mean either. The words that taught me that lesson loud and clear were *"Oh really?"* I don't usually use these words, but I certainly know full well what they mean—now. When I hear the words, I think of my podiatric surgical residency. I remember one snowy day in Philadelphia sitting near the nurse's station and waiting for the morning's attending doctor to show for an early briefing. I was exhausted, having spent much of the night before in the emergency room tending to broken bones and stitching up wounds. I was finally released from duty at three a.m. To make matters worse, I was delayed leaving the parking lot by an inch of ice covering the door handle of my car. It was an aggravating end to a hectic night. By the time I got home, it was five a.m., and I knew I was due back at the hospital for rounds at seven a.m. The attending physician had a reputation for being arrogant and condescending, and to my dismay, it soon became clear he'd set his sights on me. He starting drilling me with one medical question after another as if I were the only one at the table. I answered question after question until the one that set me over the edge: "What diagnostic test would you order to confirm osteomyelitis in a diabetic patient?"

I answered promptly and as far as I know, correctly, but he was not satisfied, and he argued with me. Having dealt with the issue in the emergency room just the night before, I was sure of my answer.

Out of frustration and sheer exhaustion, I blurted out, "Well, I don't agree with you!"

The conversation ended abruptly, and I found myself called to my residency director's office later that day. It was carefully explained to me that I must be respectful and keep my mouth shut even if I didn't agree with what was said by my attending physician. I could feel my face flush with anger, and the words slipped out of my mouth again.

"Well, I don't agree."

This time my comment was met with the raise of an eyebrow and a stern glare. I held my breath. My director's whisper housed only two words: *"Oh really?"*

What followed was not pleasant. I learned many things that day, including the fact that you don't mouth off to your attending physician—no matter how much you feel he deserves it. Most importantly, I learned that "Oh really?" is more than a simple inquisitive statement. In that instance, those words meant big trouble, run-to-the-nearest-exit type of trouble, and doing-rounds-at-five-a.m.-for-a-month type of trouble. Lesson learned!

What we say has consequences. And what we don't say has consequences that are every bit as great. Don't miss out on having a connection to the ones you love by letting illusion and self-deception get in the way of what you know you want to say.

Finding Our Zones of Comfort

I take a deep breath and am rewarded with the scent of fresh-cut grass. Exhaling, a thought comes to mind: *My life has become a repetitive cycle.* I feel vulnerable, and when I reach out, I am wounded in some manner.

My instinct beckons me to build a barrier between myself and those around me as a means of protection. Right here, right now, as I write this book, I am realizing for the first time why I put up that barrier between myself and my grandmother later in life: I was scared.

As children, we develop and grow, and we are vulnerable. We reach out to our parents for guidance and support. At seven years old, I watched my mother die in a car crash. On that day I reached out to her, and she was no longer there. It was so painful that when I sensed any kind of similar distress, I did the same thing—over and over. When I was close to my grandmother early in life, there was no reason to build a barrier—she was young, healthy, and vibrant. As time marched on, I watched her grow older, nearing what I knew was the end of her life. Instinctively that barrier went up to protect myself from the same pain I felt when my mother died. I have been putting up barriers my whole life.

So many times I have pushed someone away, only to feel lonely, isolated, and withdrawn. How many times have we said to ourselves that no one understands what we are going through? That is how I feel at this moment. The realization feels dirty as it dawns on me how often I keep people at arm's length . . . including my grandmother. Dear God, the closeness we could have shared had I opened up in my adult years, paid attention, and been there! I have kept everyone at arm's length for too long. My head has been buried in the sand.

> **"The closeness we could have shared had I opened up in my adult years, paid attention, and been there!"**

Always feeling different, I erected clever barriers throughout my life to protect myself from adversity. Always ashamed and guarded, I kept a convenient bag of tricks at my side poised to decorate the barrier so it didn't appear so obvious.

> How many of us are surrounded by people on a daily basis but still feel overtly lonely?

I see a small goose standing on a cement block—his own granite island surrounded by a sea of emerald grass. He looks lonely and isolated but also strangely secure as he gazes at the gaggle in the distance. For many of us, such an island is real, and it is sacred—a metaphorical oasis that keeps us safe and protected from the perceived dangers hidden in murky water. The deep sea, the shoreline, or our own intimate island: metaphorically speaking, these three areas can be likened to zones of comfort we set up early in our lives.

THE DEEP BLUE SEA

From my standpoint, the deep blue sea is where I keep many people for fear of being wounded. I don't regard those in this zone with hostility, judgment, or anger; they are simply not allowed close to what is important to me until they have proven worthy. I'm looking at a blade of grass near the goose. The edges are ragged and rough—reflecting my mood at this moment. It reminds me of a woman I knew during my early business endeavors. She was lovely in the beginning, and she drew me in. I recall sitting with her at a lunch meeting when she said, "So tell me about your business."

Eager to share my excitement, I divulged my ideas and dreams quickly, occasionally stopping to take a breath between thoughts. She said little through the course of the conversation—little with the exception of, "Oh really? Tell me more. You know you can trust me."

In retrospect, I did have a vague feeling of uneasiness in my stomach. I disregarded it at the time, but I know now that my gut intuition was telling me something was just not right. Regardless, I kept talking.

At the conclusion of the meeting, I paused and said with excitement, "Well! When would you like to meet next?"

My stomach did a somersault as she smiled and said wryly, "I have heard enough. No need for me to meet with you again."

I later found that she started a business after that meeting. Her tagline and website layout were replicas of my own. Lesson learned! My mind still wrestles with the same questions: *Do you trust until there is a reason not to, or do you mistrust until there is a reason to trust?*

I know what I prefer. Mistrusting those around me is not how I want to live. Figuratively speaking, the deep blue ocean is merely a holding place—an area where those who are new to me hang out and can mingle; it's a place for them to reside until I have a chance to silence my mind, collect my thoughts, and evaluate their intentions. I have found that I often need time to silence worldly noise and listen to my valuable intuition. If everything checks out, those with positive intentions are permitted close to shore. Those of whom I am unsure stay in the deep sea indefinitely.

There is no judgment in the deep blue sea. I believe there are times when people are not meant to be in close proximity where they could intentionally or unintentionally cause harm. But I realize that I have kept countless individuals in that zone for far too long. I wonder how many of us do the same. Do we do this out of doubt, or is there another reason lurking beneath the waters?

I shrug my shoulders and continue to study the blade of grass. Perhaps I am lazy. It takes work to develop and nurture a trusting relationship. It can be, in a word, exhausting. With all the day-to-day activity and responsibility, do I build tidal-wave barriers to keep people in the deep blue sea because I simply do not have the energy to nurture an amiable relationship? My psyche feels as fragmented as the blade of grass before me. There is truth in this thought. My heart cries in response. Living life in this frame of mind may seem easier, but it is a lonely way to live.

THE SHORELINE

There are times, however, when my barrier, built far offshore, comes crashing down. The weakening of the wall often starts with a kind word, a compassionate gesture, or a selfless act. As the barricade is breached, the water comes rolling toward shore, carrying a select few into the shallow water. The zone close to shore is where trust develops and meaningful conversation dominates over the mundane. Those in the shallow water are allowed closer to all we hold sacred, but the waters must be tested. Can they be trusted to proceed further?

Tiring of the blade of grass, my vision tracks to the sky, where I am delighted to see a hawk gracefully negotiating the gusts of wind off the water. Images of a woman come to mind, a vibrant soul who quickly turned into a valued friend years ago. Her kindness, compassion, and love for life are overtly apparent in all she does. She most definitely resides at my shoreline. I ponder a thought. *Do I tell her my deepest, darkest secrets?* No, I do not. I struggle with my emotions and wonder why I fail to share intimate details of my life with her.

Is it because of her? Chances are, it is not. If it had been, I would not have let that tidal-wave barrier in the deep ocean dissipate, allowing her closer to shore. Is it me? Yes, a much more likely assumption. I recognize with sadness that I am afraid to let her close for fear of what she will see. While visiting her house one day, I recall how proud she was of her dogs. I giggled in delight that day as they rolled onto their backs, exposing their tender underbellies in play. So trusting! It takes a lot for me to reveal my tender underbelly. Many of us have that same reservation.

My gaze drops from the hawk to the bay, where a sandbar just offshore comes into focus. It juts out from the shoreline, separating the calm, peaceful water close to shore from the turbulent active water in the distant sea. I realize that there are times when I build sandbars in my life much like that sandbar, a jetty in my mind that allows others to come close so as not to endure the frigid water in the deep sea, but not too close so as to expose myself in the place I feel safe. What would it take to allow others to cross and join us on our own private island? It's worth thinking about.

ISLAND OASIS

My mind screams, *Beware!* But my heart whispers that there is hidden treasure on shore meant to be shared with others. Beneath our feet is our own personal island, a paradise that serves as a tropical security blanket. It is where we allow trusted individuals close to us and where we feel safe divulging deep thoughts and intriguing feelings. It is a place where symbiotic relationships are the treasure and a location where we can feel comfortable exposing our delicate underbelly. Our island oasis is a cherished destination where judgment, hate, and jealousy do not exist. Only a select few are allowed entry; they are beckoned close on the basis of their loving support and good intentions. Trust is complete in this place, as we are confident that those to whom we grant access will never hurt us.

As I reflect upon these zones of comfort, I notice a seagull on the sandbar, standing alone, which reminds me that my grandmother was the one person I trusted completely enough to let onto my personal oasis. My cherished bond with her took years to nurture, but I let it break in my adult years. Now that I fully understand the importance of the connection, it is gone. Or is it?

My grandmother was my guardian angel—an angel who was actively by my side in my childhood years and kept an eye on me from a distance in my later years. I have no doubt that she is still my angel. I can feel her presence. Her spirit is with me; I am sure of it. I have no doubt that her love is on my side. The relationship rests with her on the hillside decorated with flowers in her honor, and I *know* the bond is tattooed on my heart and is forever resilient. Then why do I feel so lonely?

I ponder this question as I gaze out over the horizon. A mist is indeed creeping quietly over the water, forming a wall that is getting higher and building steadily. Panic mounts in my mind, and I feel anxious, isolated, uncomfortable, and claustrophobic, walled off in my own little world. I turn and again focus on the lone goose, still separate and alone on the cement block. He is not far from the crowd of geese in the distance, but he might as well be miles away.

I notice a flash of red in the middle of the geese that continue to bicker, peck, and flap their wings erratically. I fear the worst, but I find that what I see is the ball trapped helplessly in the middle of the squabble. There is a honk and a hiss and then a flutter of black wings. The ball is alone, different, and unnoticed, sitting dangerously in a sea of chaos. As the flurry among the birds escalates into a storm, the ball is struck suddenly by a flailing wing and shoots away. It's slowed down by the friction of the grass and inches to a stop. I wonder about it: it's surrounded by incessant activity yet seems isolated and all alone. I watch as the smaller goose steps off the rock, wanders over to the ball, and studies it carefully. He investigates it with a tap of the beak and begins sifting through the grass around it, taking comfort in knowing that it is not a threat. With a renewed sense of confidence, the lone bird looks up at the group in the distance and stretches his wings out in a brilliant display—a display that is largely ignored.

IGNORED

I think back to the day at the zoo with my son. I'm watching him intently as he feeds the small goat some brown pellets of food. The goat eats with vigor. They have become friends and have formed a

continued

beautiful bond. Then a sign catches my eye in the distance: *Alligator feeding at 3:00 p.m.*

Great! That will be worth seeing, I think. I glance back to my son who has his hand outstretched toward his friend. He is attempting to feed her some different brown pellets. But something has changed. The goat backs up suddenly and runs into the fence behind her with a *thud!* My son tries again. The goat runs to the corner of the pen, bleating all the way. He runs after her, clearly upset, frantically attempting to entice his small friend to return. The goat simply won't take the food. Something has obviously changed, but what? A wall has been put up suddenly, breaking the bond that they shared. My mommy-heart weeps for my son. The thrill of a newfound friendship and the heartache of abandonment—he's experiencing the sting of rejection at such an early age. Not fun . . .

I look back at my grandmother's house and see the old deck in desperate need of repair. I recall sitting with her on a deck chair, gazing out over the lawn; I can still hear the quiet murmur of the bay in the background. Such glorious days—my heart was so young, not yet shaped by the world around me. My eager mind was alive with grand anticipation of the thrilling exhilaration life's journey had in store for me. I had compassion in my heart and could see nothing less in the world. I recall my grandmother's soft hazel eyes gazing intently at me with strength and empathy. There was no one I trusted more at that moment as she urged me to feel the love in my heart, really *feel* it. Even now, because of her, I sense the love that resides deep in my soul. I recall her words: "See the world as you are right at this moment and you will never be alone."

Gazing out at the wall of mist quickly approaching, I tell myself that yes, I have lived most of my life in the presence of others yet strangely feeling alone. And yes, there have indeed been times when I felt as though I existed on my own island, lured by the promise of safety—a metaphorical oasis created just for me. I close my eyes and savor the senses in my safe place . . .

I HEAR THE WAVES BREAK AT SHORE.

I SEE THE BIRDS GLIDE IN THE WIND.

I FEEL THE SAND BENEATH MY TOES.

In analyzing my life, I have put up quite a front over the years, constructing unbreakable barriers and refusing to let my guard down. Perhaps I am using my personal island for a purpose not intended? I realize with a sigh that I have abused this safe zone. My instinct suggests that this place was intended to nurture beautiful relationships; however, I use it solely for protection. How many of us do that? It becomes an exclusive space for us, a place we go to escape from everyone and everything. It is an island surrounded by a protective ring of water. It is our personal oasis. I have so many questions . . .

What zone do the people we care about reside in?
Are they held in the deep sea or closer to shore?
What would it take for us to allow them closer?

We all, at times, put up walls to protect ourselves. Whether it is a barricade in the deep sea or a barrier at the shoreline, each is a great endeavor and takes precious energy to maintain. Unfortunately, as with many great endeavors, it comes with sacrifice.

The Cost of Comfort

I am suddenly drawn back to reality as the chattering of the geese escalates to a higher decibel. I watch as the divide between the geese and my lone feathered friend widens. Ironically, the divide between the geese calls attention to the crevasse I have created between myself and others over time. I sense the bird's isolation and loneliness as the crowd of geese migrate farther and farther away. With each honk and hiss from the crowd, the wall between the flock of geese and lone bird builds steadily. I wonder, *Is the bird really lonely, or am I simply projecting what I know is in my heart?*

I realize that it is not an easy existence for the poor little goose today on the lawn. He slowly withdraws from the remainder of the group—beaten, dominated, and forced to take refuge alone. He is clearly isolated, walled off by an invisible barrier from the rest of the crowd. His head hangs low in submission as he pokes haphazardly at the grass. I watch, captivated by his wary indifference, and I realize it is a masquerade for a glaring awareness. Although seemingly aloof, his slender head shoots up in attention every time the large goose flaps his wings in a dominant display. There is clearly a wall between the two birds, an invisible façade separating this lone dweller from the rest of the flock.

Yes, a wall is up, a barrier: His sudden indifference is a method of protecting himself, and yet it is also a way of hiding his deeper feelings and engagement with the world. Interesting . . . I wonder how many of us are guilty of the same thing. I know I am guilty. I recall an instance in my career when a woman I knew wanted nothing to do with me professionally. She did not invite me to her networking events and rejected all my attempts to collaborate on a professional level. Other colleagues noticed her dismissive response and asked me about it. My reaction to the inquiries? Aloof indifference. "I don't care. I am so busy I would not be able to participate anyway." Professionally, I put on the façade that it did not matter to me; personally, I was devastated.

I felt rejected and withdrew into my private world to protect myself emotionally. How many of us construct that deceptive wall in a haphazard attempt to protect ourselves from the outside world—to make ourselves feel normal, to integrate—but end up feeling separate, different, and alone, struggling just beneath the façade? Perhaps it would be better to ask: What does any barrier truly represent? What is its effect on our lives?

The first cool sting of the mist hits my face. A familiar wave of panic creeps closer, and I find myself having difficulty taking a breath. My chest tightens, and instinctively I look toward the heavens, searching for solitude. The thought of my lone friend on the cement block only compounds my isolation. He's looking in the direction of the others. Although he is safe from the hostility of the gaggle, his desolation is apparent as he lets out a loud honk of dismay and lowers his head in resignation as the others chatter randomly in the background. My red ball, too, now rests alone on the lawn; it is floating, deserted, on a sea of green grass. There it sits—old, alone, the red cracks in the rubber glaringly evident in its mud-packed crevices. The goose and the ball—isolated, alone, and forgotten...

FORGOTTEN

Seemingly forgotten, the people today at the zoo have faded into the background as I watch my son frantically pursue his lost goat friend from corner to corner in the animal pen. The cycle is repetitive: he offers the small brown pellets to the goat; she sniffs and draws back in obvious rejection. It is an action that clearly devastates my son; I observe his pink freckled cheeks becoming stained with tears. I watch my baby,

continued

sitting rejected in the middle of the pen, alone and isolated, wondering what went wrong. I walk to him slowly, brush away his tears, and say, "Come on, sweetheart. Let's go watch the alligator feeding."

I am surprised as he shrinks from my touch and turns away from me.

"No, Mommy, leave me alone."

My heart is breaking as I watch him walk to an empty corner of the pen and sit down by himself, isolated and alone. I find myself murmuring, "But you are certainly not forgotten . . ."

My adult heart knows that he has a choice—to withdraw and give up or to stand up and try again, one more time. What will he do? I wonder: after rejection, where does the courage come from to move forward despite the risks? Watching him sit there, his head hanging sadly, I wonder whether we are born with the determination necessary to move on in life or if it's something we develop over time.

My son suddenly gets up. He stands with his feet planted squarely on the ground and focuses intently on the goat. My questions are answered! I realize with a smile that within my little boy exists something genuinely audacious. I watch with anticipation as he looks at the goat, takes a step forward, and wipes the tears from his eyes.

Back in the present moment, I remember that tears of rejection have been something I have become familiar with over the years—rejection is a gut-wrenching feeling leading to self-doubt, withdrawal, and inevitable isolation. It is a wave that leaves us feeling unsure, vulnerable, and unloved in its wake. Considering this truth, is it any wonder that I segregate myself on my island oasis and refuse to let others close?

As the sun breaks up the mist, I feel its warmth bathe my face. I had become quite comfortable on my oasis; all my barriers were strategically in place. I had become *too* comfortable.

I'm thinking about the fact that the longer the walls remain up, the greater the risk of them becoming permanent. They can become frozen solid and so deep in the sea that no one can pass; they might turn into a persistent illusion in our minds that coaxes us into a false sense of security. Yes, with the comfort the barriers offer, they may become a permanent fixture in our psyche. With a false sense of well-being, we are less likely to venture from our safe place—and we are certainly less inclined to let anyone in. Complacency becomes the norm as we seat ourselves farther and farther from others under a phony blanket of protection.

But at what cost? With those who are held far offshore, communication is superficial at best. Inspired, insightful connections are unlikely to happen. *Is that what we want in life?*

It's not what I want in my life. That's not what life is about. When we keep others so far away from our island, from what we feel is important, we are, in essence, disconnecting. Where there is no connection, trust is nonexistent.

Once again, I see the sandbar in the distance and notice the waves lapping at its borders. What about those who reside at the shoreline in our lives? These are the select few we allow close, but not too close for comfort. With a sting of regret, I can't hide the fact that there are individuals on my shoreline who have resided there for years. They are the select few I have a glimmer of hope of letting near but not enough faith to let them in completely. At the shore there most certainly exists a barrier, an invisible wall with no bridge. Think of that bridge—connecting the gap between all we hold sacred and *what*? Excitement? Danger? At the shoreline we have the possibility of more communication, a higher degree of connection, and enhanced trust—but we need to look at our hesitation to open up completely.

• • •

What makes up an ideal relationship? Can that quintessential liaison be ideal if we hold loved ones in the symbolic sea or on an imaginary shoreline? If I am honest, it takes an act of God for me to let individuals onto my oasis. In my life, there have only been a handful of people I have allowed island-close. I realize today that whom we let in is a highly personal decision, not to be swayed by the opinions of others. Standing on that island, gazing at those on the shoreline, I know that I do have the tools necessary to build that bridge, but I hesitate every single time. Why? Fear. Fear of being hurt. Fear of losing myself. Fear of the unknown.

Deep in my heart I know the one thing that overcomes fear. It is love—love and the light that accompanies it. Love comes in many forms. There is the love for that which surrounds us, for ourselves, and for those close to us. All are equally important. With those for whom I have built a bridge in my life, the communication and the sense of connection is greater than anything I had ever imagined. I am willing to bet that many of us have experienced the thrill of sharing our personal oasis with the right person at some point in our lives. Being exposed in this fashion is both terrifying and exhilarating at the same time. The act is so scary that I often find myself paralyzed when it comes to laying the first plank in the bridge. I desperately want to build that bridge, not just for the few but for many others. I wonder, *Where does the courage come from to bridge the gap and take a chance once again?*

Eye on Adventure

Standing on the lawn today, I notice a child with a loaf of bread in her hand. She has come to feed the geese. I'm surprised at how quickly the hoard of birds surround her, honking and hissing. The smaller goose stays at a safe distance, curiously observing as the child throws a chunk of bread high in the air. The piece lands, and one goose from the flock picks it up and runs; the remainder of the group chase after it in what looks like a crazy football game. The crowd moves off, leaving the lone goose behind, but I am intrigued to find that he is no longer alone. He has found himself a friend—a female goose. They both stand and look up at the young girl who is now giggling as she watches the flock running in the distance.

The goose in possession of the bread is now running in zigzag sprints while the remaining players struggle to keep up. The girl looks down at the duo at her feet, smiles, and reaches into her pants pocket. She draws out a second loaf of bread that she breaks into pieces, a reward for those who are patient, open, and accepting. The two geese have resisted the urge to run off in a frenzy with the rest of the flock and now stand at her feet politely, wings brushing up against one another and looking up expectantly. There is no hissing or commotion. There is no danger or animosity, just comfort being in each other's presence. They stand together preparing to enjoy what fate has extended to them.

In the scuffle, the group of geese runs over the old red ball in a whirlwind of webbed feet, and somehow the ball is propelled skyward across the yard. It drops and rolls and comes to a slow stop at the edge of an embankment; below lie jagged rocks

"With regard to relationships in our lives, I can't help but wonder if being on the edge is precisely what we need."

and unforgiving waves. The ball is alone, on the edge, positioned to fall to its demise. I watch as the wind jostles it from left to right, teasing it as it gets closer to the precipice. With Grandma gone, I, too, feel as though I am teetering on the edge, alone, and anticipating my demise. I feel out of control, but I look past the dangerous rocks to the horizon. Beyond the rocks and waves is something oddly exciting and promising. The water goes on for what seems like miles, whispering promises of a rewarding journey. I smile. With regard to relationships in our lives, I can't help but wonder if being on the edge is precisely what we need.

Perhaps we all need a little push in the right direction. Once positioned there, we may feel the urge to take action by the pressure to make a choice. Relationships can fail or they can flourish. The choice is ours. We can let our relationships fail, or we can look deep within and find the courage necessary to share our island oasis with those we love. I watch as the ball becomes still on the hillside, vulnerable to the wind's next breath. Vulnerability is a scary concept, but sometimes with fear comes the thrill of adventure. Oh yes, I think I am finally ready to take a chance in my life. I turn and gaze fondly at the lone goose and his newfound friend. They stand together, quietly honking, happy, and clearly enjoying the last morsels of bread. They are quite unlike the crazy crowd of geese in the distance, wings flapping frantically, fighting for the hunk of bread. Oh yes, I am finally ready to build that bridge. I am determined . . .

DETERMINED

Determined is a good way to describe my son's demeanor as he squares off with the goat at the zoo once again. He offers yet another pellet and is again rejected.

I hurt for him as his shoulders drop in defeat. He slides down onto a nearby tree stump and looks up at me with eyes filled with tears.

What *is* the problem? It can't be who he is. His child's heart is filled with nothing but love and compassion. Perhaps, just maybe—could it be what he is offering?

As I ponder the thought of my son's past plight, I am quickly drawn back to the present moment by thoughts of offering and rejection. A concept ricochets through my head: in life, perhaps our relationships are not as strong as they should be—not because of who we are but because of what we are offering. Think about it. Are we offering a hand onto our oasis by building a bridge, or are we sabotaging the efforts of those who mean well by continually repairing the wall of resistance? I wonder how many friends and loved ones I have kept at sea over the years who didn't need to be there. I speculate about how many caring people have given up on me as I left them negotiating the waves at the shoreline for too long. *What would it take to build that bridge to the shore and offer a daiquiri on the beach to the ones I care about?*

Refuse to Be Trapped

What choice do we have? We know we are strong. We are tougher than we give ourselves credit for. Despite what people say, despite self-defeating thoughts, we have something to offer, and it is valuable and powerful. We not only have a right to break through our restrictive barriers—we have an obligation.

> **"It's time to stop beating ourselves up."**

We owe it to ourselves to take a good, long look at those barricades and see them for what they really are: an obstacle to forward growth, a prison cell that traps us. I refuse to be trapped by anything or anyone, and that includes myself. I shake my head in bewilderment. Shame on me! Who would have thought that the person responsible for my current isolation is staring at me in the mirror every morning?

Now is the time to sink or swim—to break or bounce. But first I must look at one crucial factor: I must look within myself and realize with certainty that I have something of value to offer. All of us must acknowledge that what resides within is good, genuine, and worthy of true love. What resides within is magnificent and a brilliant treasure when offered from the heart. It's time to stop beating ourselves up. I firmly believe that within all of us lies an alluring maze of complex artistry, a creative array of thoughts, feelings, and ambitions that make us unique. We must have confidence in this maze and use our newfound courage to put the first planks in the bridge in place. We are all brilliant beacons that, when given proper credit, shine. The prerequisite in building that bridge is to realize that we are strong individuals worthy of true love. When that message is internalized, we can't help but see the world in a positive light. Think about it. When that light is realized and offered to others unconditionally, they will draw close. Bathed in the light of awareness, we are never truly alone.

For the first time in weeks, I feel a glimmer of hope in my heart. When we recognize the beauty within ourselves and see the world through those eyes, it is easier to know the ones who are true in our lives. Intuition then lights the path for those who are genuine. As I reflect back on the woman who stole my company's idea and the consultant who took liberties with my business, I realize something important: like attracts like. Up until now there has been a degree of darkness in my heart. That darkness has cloaked the natural light within and attracted negativity from my surroundings. Standing here right now, the truth is all too clear: with love and light in our hearts, we are more likely to attract those with true and honest intentions in theirs. It is as simple as that. If our vision is true, we will see sincerity in the heart of most.

"Bathed in the light of awareness, we are never truly alone."

We have a choice. Our relationships can live or die. The wall can remain intact, or it can come crashing down. The choice is ours. That choice depends on one important factor: a quality we were born with, a quality that society constantly attempts to strip us of slowly, over time. We must learn to truly trust again, developing trust in others. But more importantly, we need to build trust in ourselves.

Trust and Heal

How do we develop, sustain, or regain trust in others? This is a question I have struggled with for years. Glancing back and forth between the calm couple foraging through the grass before me and the frenzied flock in the distance, it occurs to me that many factors are involved in establishing trust in a relationship. Why do we lose trust in those around us? For me, it has a lot to do with the wounds I have endured throughout the course of my life. Some of those wounds are still open. I realize with certainty that my personal wounds have left me scared and in pain. It is that fear and discomfort that has left me incapable of bridging the gap between myself and those I love. Perhaps building bridges has a lot to do with healing festering wounds.

We've all heard it said that all wounds eventually heal. That may be true, but I think we can also all agree that those wounds often leave scars more painful than the original cuts.

It occurs to me that healing wounds of the past boils down to five important factors:

Faith

Expectations

Beliefs

Bondage

Moxie

I grin. Seems like a crazy combination, but it is something Grandma taught me over the years. Together these factors form a tool capable of demolishing persistent barricades.

FAITH: SEE THE LIGHT

I look skyward and see the sun's brilliant beams bursting through the clouds. Grandma always loved the warmth of the sun. I can see the rays spilling over the bay in a brilliant prism. Funny—we don't just hope the sun comes up in the morning, warms our hearts through the day, and calms our spirits in the evening; we have faith that it will. It will, precisely as it always has.

In a similar fashion, we must have faith in our relationships with others. There are always so many questions when we think about bringing down that all-important barrier out in the sea: *Will they be good to me? Will I be good to them? Will they accept what they see?*

Eradicating personal barriers in our lives is certainly an evolving process. How can I possibly have the faith necessary to let someone close to me if I do not have the confidence first in what resides deep in my heart? Through years of school, training, and work, these questions have repeatedly resurfaced in my mind: *Am I good enough? Will I disappoint them? How will I deal with yet another rejection?*

I don't remember having those thoughts as a child, but as an adult I most certainly do. It is sometimes easier as time marches on to keep people swimming far from what I hold sacred. Forever swimming in the deep blue sea—how exhausting that must be! How many people have given up on me as they grew tired of waiting? What my grandmother always taught me is that I must have faith, and that faith and self-esteem are intimately related. As the sun shines brightly overhead, it becomes crystal clear; faith in the treasure that resides deep at our core is essential.

Faith is a gift. It starts first and foremost with getting to know ourselves, acknowledging the wounds we have incurred over time and what they have done to our lives. In Grandma's own way, she often tried to tell me this. As a child, I always welcomed the light, since I was afraid of the imaginary monster that lurked in my closet after dark. It's ironic—as an adult, I seem to be afraid of something entirely different. I am afraid of the light within myself, the one thing capable of illuminating my existence or able to serve as a beacon for others to move closer to me. We must see the light that shines from within and realize it is worthy of our undying faith. After all, if we don't have confidence in our own internal beacon, who will?

We show faith in ourselves by setting clear goals. It is imperative that we acknowledge our successes and give credit where credit is due. More importantly, we must put failure into perspective. Faith in oneself and perceived failure are intimately connected. For many of us, when we think that we have failed, we lose faith in our abilities. The way I see it, failure is merely a tool by which we learn life's lessons all too well. When the concept of failure is put into perspective, we are better able to acknowledge the wounds incurred in life. With positive attention, wounds heal and scars soften. Only then are we able to look through the pain and have faith in the good that resides within our hearts. Relationships flourish in the light of abundance harbored within us all. We must have faith in that light; we must have faith in ourselves.

EXPECTATIONS: SEE THE BEACON

As the sun's rays bounce off the water in the bay today, I notice a lone piece of driftwood not far from shore. It is having difficulty negotiating the waves. I witness as it's being pushed closer, only to be drawn back out into deep water by the relentless undertow. I sigh; the act of pushing and pulling seems to be a common theme in day-to-day life, a constant tug-of-war that threatens to leave us isolated and alone. Standing solitary on our metaphorical oasis, we may witness the determined few starting the journey to shore, drawn to the light in our hearts that beacons to them softly. Like the driftwood, they may find the water rough and the current strong, roughened by day-to-day drama and strengthened by internal conflict. Years of lessons learned and wounds incurred have left our personal insecurity in its tumultuous wake, making it difficult

for individuals to venture closer. Our longing for love and companionship ignites the light from within and ultimately beckons lone survivors
closer, while fear, insecurity, and apprehension throw a cloak over the
light that dampens our internal beacon. I wonder how many survivors
become confused and inevitably lost when that happens. The result?
The current draws them farther and farther away. We watch as some are
pulled under, into the blue-gray depths of oblivion, to be forgotten forever, while still others are kept at sea for yet another sentence of solitude.

Some of us exist on personal island oases, and we watch carefully as
those kept outside the boundary are drawn to our internal light. As they
come closer, we become insecure, which dampens the light within. This
process unknowingly sabotages the weary, who are unaware of one important factor: expectations. Perhaps we expect too much from others (which,
in many cases, pushes them away) and too little of ourselves, which leads
to personal insecurity and withdrawal. Insecurity and withdrawal serve
as relentless storms masking our internal light and making it difficult for
others to see the beacon before them. Even a meaningful relationship may
find it difficult to withstand these stormy conditions. As a result, we sit in
the darkness lonely and insecure, watching as the gap widens between our
oasis and those in the deep blue sea. We may soon find ourselves alone to
nurse the wounds incurred over the course of time.

We have all been wounded. Emotional and physical trauma seem all
too common in today's extreme society. I gaze at the bay and contemplate an intriguing thought. Wounds and expectations seem to be intimately related, often developing a curious relationship of their own. If I
am honest with myself, there are times when I am all too eager to wear
phony cuts and bruises like a badge of honor. That badge worn on our
chest masks the light from within and dampens the extraordinary light
of our internal beacon. I know that I am not alone. I have seen many in
my life wear that badge proudly and expect others to acknowledge and
honor the symbol in what is often a dark, foolish game. For some, if

expectations are not met and that badge is not honored, the expectant party may be left in the water negotiating the waves. I know that for me, relaying my life drama to others often goes beyond constructive communication; it turns into an obsession in which I act out the pain over and over in an insane cycle that never ends. This ultimately keeps my wounds open and fresh. They are never allowed to heal. It is a process that is incredibly painful.

Some of our wounds are housed deep in an underwater vault locked by fear. It is then that our internal beacon becomes dangerously dim. We lock the vault tightly, careful never to reveal its contents for fear of being judged, criticized, or persecuted. Oh yes, I have been there. Those wounds held deep in our minds are toxic and serve no greater purpose than to erode a hole in the soul, a hole through which our self-esteem seeps slowly into the darkness. So sad, isn't it? For many of us, the more self-confidence we lose, the less confident we become in our abilities, and sadly we expect less and less of ourselves.

I can't help but think that to truly heal our bruises, we must realize that our open wounds dampen our internal beacon and keep those we love at sea. And the more we expect others to commiserate without accepting their constructive advice, the greater the strength of the undertow. When our expectations of others are too great, the light dims and survivors become lost. We then risk ending up cold and lonely on an oasis meant to be shared.

Perhaps a viable option would be to ignite our internal beacon by identifying open wounds directly, acknowledging them, and dealing with them quickly and promptly. When wounds are healed, pain is released, and scars soften. Our light shines brightly. When our past cuts and bruises are healed, we stop setting unrealistic expectations regarding those in the deep blue sea. We no longer have reason to expect so much from others. Guided by instinct, we are then more inclined to turn inward toward our own light and expect more from within. Oh yes, that is what we must do.

WITHIN, THERE IS SO MUCH MORE

We must understand that what we have gone through in our lives, positive and negative, has made us strong. We are vastly capable of healing our own wounds. When we heal our internal selves, our light is liberated. Strength and courage become a badge of honor as we are brutally honest with ourselves. Honesty is the prerequisite to trust. Once we expect good things from ourselves, our confidence radiates to the world. It is that radiance, that warmth, that serves as a beacon, lighting the path for loved ones to follow.

BELIEVE: HEAR THE HORN

I glance back at my grandmother's house, watching as the light from the water forms a brilliant prism that bounces off the windows and explodes in all different directions. It is gorgeous, dazzling. It is magnificent because my mind and heart have molded the image into one beautiful portrait.

Today the beauty before me goes beyond mere perception. My mind perceives elegance, but instinct tells me that to truly experience exquisite beauty, it must be felt at the level of the heart. When someone or something touches our hearts, it impacts our lives deeply and is remembered forever. I don't simply

"Our beliefs become our reality."

think the scene before me today is beautiful; I *believe* that it is. The scene before me fills my heart with joy and will be etched into my memories forever. In many respects, our beliefs become our reality. We must believe.

TO SEE IT, WE MUST BELIEVE IT

I often feel as though I have spent most of my life desperately trying to find someone or something to believe in. An entity to lean on, a figure on a pedestal who will offer me the all-important validation I yearn for. Many of us require external acknowledgment in order to feel proud, honorable, or worthy. Looking out over the water, I realize that my quest for outside validation has never been truly successful over the years. One relationship after another has disappointed me in some manner. But why? My thoughts return to my grandmother's words. Perhaps the problem is not this person I wanted to place on a pedestal. More than likely, the problem is my beliefs and thought patterns. Right here, right now, I realize something vitally important: I haven't been looking in the right place for hope. Hope for all of us exists, but it does not reside in the people that surround us—or the circumstances we stumble upon. Hope resides *within* us. To see it, we must believe it.

There is something admirable in all of us, of that I am sure. When we believe in what resides within and trust ourselves enough to look beyond the scars incurred in life, an amazing thing happens: we begin to listen to what our souls are whispering. As we become aware, we begin to see the vibrancy and energy within ourselves. An excitement surfaces, announcing itself in a triumphant wake-up call—a beautiful signal to others that we finally believe in who we are. When we see ourselves in that light, how can we not see the world as warm, inviting, and full of mystery and adventure? For the first time, we find the determination to truly open our eyes and focus on those people treading water, their heads just above the surface.

Deep in the water are many who truly believe in who we are and what we stand for. That belief keeps them swimming steadily, slowly making progress toward shore. But we must remember that they also have something of value to offer. An exhilarating thought: by joining us on our oasis, our joint value multiplies into a tidal wave of possibilities. As the excitement builds, anticipating this beautiful unity, many of us find our voices. That voice is like a foghorn on a misty night, carrying a whisper with the wind to all who are receptive to the call. We have a right to be heard. By believing in what we stand for, we uncover the ability to see the good in others and know inherently what it means to lift them to new heights. We must learn to believe in ourselves and also to believe in others. A strong belief and the hope that ensues serve as a beckoning call, a signal that it is time to demolish personal barriers, welcome the bond of companionship, and live the life that we want and deserve.

ESCAPE: FEEL THE FREEDOM

The burst of light reflected off the window fans out in a magnificent display, but then it's gone. Recalling many of my early relationships, I remember the dazzling feeling of something new and exciting, a pleasure that was soon threatened by the danger of fear and insecurity. I wonder how many of us have let brilliant relationships sink to the depths of oblivion in the face of danger, finding ourselves dominated by uncertainty and self-doubt. With regard to companionship, I have often held my breath waiting for "the next shoe to drop"—an unseen danger lying in wait, lurking in the deep water. Feeling hunted, we may find it easier to stay seemingly safe but certainly not secure on our oasis. We become bound by the perception of danger, held hostage on an island whose beauty is yet to be discovered. It may seem safe and secure all by ourselves, but I wonder, *Is it really?*

For me, that island has become a deep, dark place. Instead of standing bathed by the warmth of the sun, welcoming others to shore, I retreat to the depths of a jungle trapped by darkness and doubt. I stand here today in the yard my grandmother loved so much and realize I was not closer to her for one reason only: I was terrified. I was trapped in a maze of life's vines and thorns, desperately attempting to find a way out, all the while terrified of what I would find once I did.

I am still struggling to get out of that place, trapped in the dark, looking for a way out. It is not unusual to be trapped in ghostly bondage. I have seen family, friends, and patients trapped by painful wounds that refuse to let go of their hearts, wrapped up in a sadistic bondage that seems impossible to escape. Our minds work desperately, analyzing every scenario in a futile attempt to work our way out of a constrictive black hole where actions are dictated by the ego, an entity that thrives on fear and insecurity. For those of us bound by uncertainty, bondage is suffocating, leaving us chained to the past and unable to enjoy the present.

Contemplating that thought, I stare at the windows of the house, which are now flat and dark, lifeless in the absence of light. It occurs to me that escaping the confines of fear and insecurity lies in one important concept: today. Living today—not in the past, not in the future, and certainly not with the ego. Today is where attention is meant to be; it is where true freedom lies. Where there is attention, there is light. We must take our fears and write them down—post them on our bathroom mirrors if we have to. Attend to each and every one each and every day. Oh yes, where there is attention, there is light; where there is light, darkness does not exist. Dangers lurking beneath the water are no longer ominous; they become issues not worthy of another thought, simply

> **"We must take our fears and write them down—post them on our bathroom mirrors if we have to."**

something to be dealt with promptly. Where we put our attention is where we will see the results. We deserve to live a life free from life's thorns and vines, and we mustn't allow fear and insecurity to dominate. Let us walk to the water's edge in the warmth of the sun and feel the freedom for ourselves once again. As our bondage is broken, we can feel confident in extending our arms in a genuine welcome. It just might be the sign all swimmers have been waiting for.

MOXIE: A TASTE OF TENACITY

I glance at the sun overhead and then down over the vast expanse of water before me. If I look closely, I can faintly see remnants of color dancing across the water. Reflecting back on the funeral today, I recall my father's solemn face as he gazed at my grandmother's grave. My heart hurts in remembrance of his demeanor today. Right now I feel hollow, much like an empty shell. There is nothing left after today. Or is there?

My attention is drawn to the child, still feeding the two lone geese, and my mind suddenly bursts into activity. Images of me with those I love flash through my mind one by one: children playing, family gatherings, friends laughing.

You know what? In each and every image that pops into mind today, I am *smiling*. Oh yes, there is something left inside of me, remnants of who I really am, fragments that I suddenly realize are the sparks that ignite my spirit. They have guts, grit, and spunk—tenacious remnants at the core of who I am that have been suppressed for far too long.

There is a reason why I am afraid to let others close to me. I have been judged, pushed around, and taken advantage of for far too long. I am tired.

> **"I have been judged, pushed around, and taken advantage of for far too long."**

How many of us feel the same way—tired of day-to-day drama but afraid to show it? I say that it is time. Time to stand up and show the world what we are made of. It's time to develop moxie.

Moxie in life comes from bringing forth the fortitude, courage, and stamina that reside at the core of our being. It is time not only to live on the edge, but also to thrive. Moxie allows us to burst through barriers even if we are not sure what shadows lurk under the water's surface.

FORTITUDE

In life it is often difficult to push forward when faced with adversity; it takes strength and a significant amount of prowess. Looking back at the tumultuous moments of my life, I realize that much of the negativity was linked to one primary factor: judgment. Judgment dictates our actions when we favor the voices of others over our own. *We must have the fortitude to withstand judgment.* Judgment is the island's worst enemy, an entity that inflicts painful wounds. When scarred and in pain, our protective instinct takes over, prompting us to build and strengthen the barriers that block the faithful from joining us on our island oasis. I have worked hard to heal the wounds incurred in my life. We are all different, but we indeed have wounds. Judgment only serves to infect wounds, strengthen barriers, and prompt us to lose sight of the good that resides with all of us. Developing the emotional and physical strength to face those who judge and put them in their place is essential. It is time to stand up and say enough is enough.

COURAGE

There are some individuals who elevate their sense of self-worth by demeaning the esteem of others. These individuals feed on one person after another, attacking with ruthless words and derogatory comments. On the receiving end of this barrage of negativity, many feel worthless

continued

and depleted at the end of the day. *We must summon the courage to resist being governed by those with a narcissistic flare.* These individuals must not be allowed to force their opinions upon us; they must know that they have no say in how our lives are run. Those whose criticisms are only meant to crush and destroy are meant to be left at sea. We must, however, resist the urge to use this experience to strengthen our barrier so no one can pass. Not all individuals push and demand.

STAMINA

Looking back through times in my life, there have been people who acted much like an ocean wave on a stormy day. They are beautifully passive from afar, drawing time and attention, then come rolling in fast, striking us to the ground with their deceptive, aggressive force. When this happens, it is imperative that we seek solid ground and stand firm. *We must have stamina.* Resilience is necessary to resist those in the water who are both passive and aggressive. This type of person presents problem after problem without offering a solution, in most cases with a self-serving motive in mind. Engaging in activity of this type proves to be an insane cycle ending with skyrocketing stress levels and plummeting energy. Many of us are true to our heart and want to help others, but there comes a point when the best way to help someone is to insist that they help themselves first.

Oh yes, a taste of tenacity is essential in attracting and nurturing a healthy relationship. By igniting our spirit with a hefty dose of fortitude, courage, and stamina, we become confident in the fact that we indeed have the moxie to keep ourselves out of harm's way. With that, heart and mind alike are encouraged to take the barricade down, build a bridge, and let the true at heart pass.

> **"Let the true at heart pass."**

Build the Bridge

When it comes to healing wounds and pursuing healthy relationships, sometimes small strides are easier to manage than large leaps of faith. The hissing and commotion from the large group of geese is securely in the background now. I smile—the lone goose is no longer lonely. I watch as he and his friend waddle off toward the beach, their tail feathers bobbing back and forth to the accompaniment of happy honks of contentment. My heart sings as they wander onto the beach side by side, secure in each other's presence. My mind searches for a forgotten thought and quickly finds it. *Where is my ball?* I look around and see it on the embankment edge. Like all of us at times in our life, the ball is on the edge of something, but it is strangely secure. Behind it is the safety of the grass; before it lies the vast horizon—risky yet exciting. Much like our relationships in life. What adventure will the ball have next? My mind wanders. *Adventure . . .*

ADVENTURE

This frustrating adventure was not what my son had in mind today at the zoo. I watch as he faces off with the female goat, determined to work out their differences. He quickly approaches the animal, who

continued

is now in the corner. I watch as he looks down at the ground, bends over, and stops. What is he doing? As soon as the thought escapes, I see him kneel down and scoop pellets off the ground. I gasp.

The brown pellets he is offering are the animal's droppings! I hurry over to my son as the goat withdraws again in disgust. I touch his arm and give him a can full of real food. The big blue eyes open wide with excitement, showing me that he clearly understands his error. He offers the animal the food, and it rushes in close and eats contently. Success! Friends once again.

Dynamic images of my son's inquisitive blue eyes fill me with hope. The goat's rejection had nothing to do with who my son was as an individual. It had everything to do with what he was unknowingly offering. When rejected, many take the aversion to mean that there is something wrong with us personally. Perhaps it is less about what is wrong with us and instead has to do with what we are offering others. When faced with adversity, it may not be wise to react with withdrawal and fear. Reactions of this nature only deepen wounds and prevent them from healing. A more productive solution may be to look at the situation and evaluate what we are offering emotionally.

There are sailboats on the horizon. The friendly goose duo lingers on the beach. Rejection is a sensitive subject. My mind wanders from thought to thought: the geese, my son, and the ball. For the first time in years, I don't feel so alone. Grandma's words again echo in my heart: "See the world as you are right at this moment and you will never be alone." The meaning of her words has never been clearer. You see, the key to bouncing and not breaking under the perils of life lies in *healing wounds of the past*. There is something special deep within all of us. There is love in our hearts that lights the path, serving as a signal to all who have been waiting for us that it is time to come home. It is that light, that love, that will ultimately attract those who are meant to be close.

The agony and suffering that accompany open wounds are like sharks in the ocean, scavenging and devouring all in their path. We must release anger. I realize with sorrow in my heart that right here, right now, I am angry at my grandmother for leaving—leaving before I had time to say goodbye. But the rage is most certainly misdirected, isn't it? Deep in my heart, I know the only person I am furious with is myself. Once I'm finally being honest, I feel the tension in my shoulders release; my heart's load has lightened, and my mind's flexibility has increased. I suddenly feel better equipped to bend with what life has in store for me in the future. In the end, when wounds are healed, there is only love and light. When we realize this, it is then time to live!

When we face and acknowledge the cuts and bruises of the past, we grow. We develop. When we evolve, those barriers between us and the people at sea start to crumble. We learn how incredibly important it is to build bridges instead of barriers. I realize while looking up at today's beautiful blue sky that the person hiding behind the wounds is not someone to be feared. Existing within us is a treasure not to be hidden from the world.

There is good within all of us, genuine compassion and love that is waiting to be recognized. We have much to offer the world. The world has much to offer us. We must build that bridge and welcome the true at heart onto our oasis. Let us celebrate the valor that is in all of us. When we see ourselves that way, the world changes. When we are at peace with our pain, there is no longer anything to hide from. We become comfortable being alone with ourselves, as there is no longer a battle in our hearts. I smile at the irony. *I don't feel lonely now that I am OK with being alone.*

It makes entire sense now. When our wounds are not laid to rest, we hide behind an invisible barrier. When we do this, what the world sees is not who we are but a reflection of the desperate emotions escaping in the form of emotional waste. That garbage takes many forms: jealousy, hatred, and violence, to name a few. This is certainly a point to ponder.

Many of us intentionally or unintentionally offer this garbage to others, causing them to draw back in disdain and mistrust. My face flushes in embarrassment as things I have said in my past flash erratically through my mind. "I love what you have done with your business," when I am secretly jealous of the progress someone has made. "She is such a lovely person," when I am really thinking how dreadfully awful she was to my face. "Um . . . I'm not sure how I got that bruise on my leg," when I know the bruise resulted from opening the door in rage only to have it ricochet back and smack me in the leg. Some would argue that while these statements represent half-truths, what someone doesn't know won't hurt them. *Right?* Wrong.

On an intuitive level they *do* know. Scraps in the form of half-truths are felt on a deeper level and will most certainly come to light. Sooner or later others realize that we are offering them emotional garbage and react with disdain and mistrust. If we find ourselves lonely, perhaps it's time to look at the anguish within us. In many cases, what is at our core is not what others reject—it is the emotional waste we offer out of fear. Years of my own unhealed wounds have led to self-doubt and insecurity.

> **"Scraps in the form of half-truths are felt on a deeper level and will most certainly come to light."**

I recall a day years ago when I was in the middle of divorce proceedings with my now ex-husband. I was terrified, hurt, and confused. Deep down I truly didn't want to hurt him, but out of fear came anger. From telephone calls to courtrooms, mental scrap in the form of anger and resentment infiltrated my life, forming a barrier that made resolution of conflict impossible. Not only that, my anger also seeped into my relationships with family and friends, making it difficult for them to help me. I realize that over the years, I've been rejected after I have pushed my emotional waste on others. Destructive words or insincere actions serve no other purpose than to push others away.

Emotional waste is an interesting concept. Negativity, narcissism, judgment—the list goes on. What is the purpose? Garbage of this nature can have no other consequence than to drive others farther and farther away from our oasis. When we offer trash, we get trash back in return. It is as simple as that.

The key is to let go of emotional baggage and acknowledge the beauty within us and the brilliance that surrounds us. Beauty is magnified when it is shared with the right person. When we acknowledge this, we radiate confidence. That radiance serves as a conduit, a bridge that others use to join us in paradise.

I stand here today, in the brilliant sun, feeling a bit more pliable. My quiet reflection has been, in a word, therapeutic. The mist over the water has dissipated, revealing an expansive horizon decorated by wisps of white clouds. The group of geese in the distance has taken flight, carrying their bickering with them. I watch the two lone geese contently wade into the bay. Their tail feathers bob up and down as they swim off in sync.

IN SYNC

My little boy and his found-again friend are certainly in sync today at the zoo. My son looks up proudly and beams at me as the goat nudges

continued

his leg, clearly expecting more food. Demanding little thing—the goat, that is. My son is ecstatic and hands her one pellet after another. This time he is careful to take the offering from the cup in his hand and not the ground. I watch as the goat brushes against his leg one last time. Yes, they are friends indeed. Today the best has come out in both of them. As they wander off into the corner together, I realize that the wall of mistrust has been obliterated, and my little boy has been welcomed onto an oasis of contentment.

Love and Be Loved, Support and Be Supported, Listen and Be Listened To

If my ball could feel emotions, today it would feel contentment. I remember the thrill I felt as a child when I kicked it high in the air. Today it is perched high, but high on an embankment. Interaction with today's guests has pushed it into new, exciting territory—thrilling territory that may not have otherwise been explored. Its journey will continue.

> We all deserve that journey. We may sit on our island, an oasis we hold sacred, but how many of us yearn for the warmth of an engaging conversation and the comfort of a hand extended in friendship? We are strong, stronger than we know. We are strong, confident individuals who bring so much beauty into the world. Oh yes, we do. True inner strength comes from healing our battle wounds first and foremost.

It is essential, however, that we follow by developing genuine love and acceptance for who we are as individuals. We have got to be determined. Determined to love and be loved, support and be supported, listen and be listened to.

Contemplating that thought, I feel an overwhelming sense of

encouragement fill my heart. On our island, we must strive to inspire and be inspired every single day.

Joseph F. Newton expressed it well when he said, "People are lonely because they build walls instead of bridges."

It is true. Many of us do not build bridges because we are not comfortable with who we are. We still see ourselves as wounded victims acting out a role in an old movie we can replay over and over again. Standing here today, I have made a decision: *Not me. No way. Not anymore.*

I stand here today with visions of my metaphorical oasis surrounding me. Why don't I build that bridge? I am willing to bet that it is easier than I think. Our journey is effortless only if we have faith in the light within us. It is essential that we let go of unrealistic expectations and always believe there is a common ground. I have spent most of my life afraid of making mistakes. In my mind, I was not allowed to make a mistake, and if I did, it meant I had failed. This is a burden I placed *on myself.* I recall striving for perfection in my grades year after year in podiatric medical school. I sacrificed friends and even my health to maintain an impeccable GPA. Looking back, was it worth it? I am responsible for the shackles that bind me. I have no doubt that within each and every one of us exists the ability to escape the

> "I am responsible for the shackles that bind me."

bonds that stifle us and to approach the world with a spark of tenacity. Look out, world, a healthy dose of moxie is coming your way! Oh yes—this is incredibly exciting.

Relationships that blossom in our inner light are protected by the muscular arms of courage. Courage is what moves us closer. You see, rewarding relationships are within our reach, but we must be brave enough to assist others out of the sea and into our hearts. It is time to invite people in close. I am not talking shoreline-close; I am talking island-close. We must destroy the barricades in our minds and build bridges into our hearts. Island-close is the beautiful oasis at the core of our being where trust is paramount and love flows freely. It may take awhile to develop that fortitude; we must work at it. The courage to let our relationships shine, flourish, develop, and build exists deep within us, far beyond the wounds sustained in life. Happiness exists for all of us, of that I am sure. It's time to sip a daiquiri on the island together.

Part Four

PERFECTLY IMPERFECT

"The clearest way into the universe is
through a forest wilderness."

—John Muir

A Flicker of Light: Our Flawed Ideals of Perfection

As I stand in the middle of Grandma's lush, expansive lawn, a flicker of light in the bushes catches my eye. I look closely and see a beer can, its shiny aluminum surface reflecting the sun's rays. I catch sight of its faded white label and blue lettering. In an instant, I'm transported back to festive family gatherings where beer cans were the sign of a happy event. Examining it closely, I see that it's crushed on one end, while the opposite end shows no sign of damage. I suddenly feel claustrophobic and confined, as if a vice has clamped my chest. It's difficult to breathe. I'm scared.

So much looms before me: building a business, being a mother, maintaining friendships, and running a household are at the forefront of my mind. I have struggled my entire life with the concept of perfection and imperfection. I have always been driven toward absolute excellence in every aspect of my life. I had to be the perfect student, the perfect wife, the perfect mother, the perfect businesswoman, but now I feel much like that can: exhausted and depleted.

My mind and body are crushed, but my heart struggles to remain intact. It's the old perfect–imperfect conflict. I find myself desperately searching for a way to make sense of what my life has become. As one task after another looms on the horizon, my mind argues that the best way to deal with things is to simply not deal with them. My heart shouts that running from things will only prolong and worsen my misery.

As I raise my head, I am rewarded by the warmth of the sun on my face. I close my eyes and smell the sweet scent of the fir trees; I hear the whisper of the wind through the branches. But a sudden and intrusive call of a blackbird highjacks my thoughts and sends them tumbling through a maze of images that ends with the vision of my grandmother's gravesite. I'm struggling hard to erase the pain the vision causes, but my mind remains steadfast in binding me to the events surrounding her death. The tears, guilt, and loneliness are memories I want to get away from and forget.

But two sights take my mind away for a moment. One is a hawk, and the other is my childhood ball. The hawk is gliding silently above the treetops. The bird is brilliant, beautiful, and twisting and turning with each gust of wind. My heart says that the incredible creature is free to negotiate the waves of the wind, while my mind argues that the bird is desperate to escape its confines.

My ball is perched precariously on the edge of an embankment. The sun is merciless, beating down on the faded rubber; vines encircle its base and creep over the top, keeping it tethered to the ground. Below the embankment, I catch sight of the jagged rocks. The grass around the ball sways back and forth cunningly, teasingly pushing the ball closer to the edge with each gust of wind.

Choosing Adventure

It's interesting to me that, like us, the ball has a choice of paths to take at this stage in its journey. It can stay where it is, seemingly safe but painstakingly confined—or, if enticed by the wind, it can venture out of its den, taste momentary freedom, and then meet its demise on the rocks below. I take in the scene—the ball, the embankment, the rocks below, and farther away, I see the blissful bay with cool, dark water and gentle waves. I imagine how comforting it would be for the ball to be cradled in the tranquil waves, undulations taking it to thrilling places and exhilarating experiences. We all want that, don't we? I know I do. But to achieve success, my ball must bypass the rocks in order to embark on its journey. But how? Do we go around danger . . . or through it to freedom?

I make another futile attempt to erase the painful memory of my grandmother's grave, and even though the vision is gone, the scars that bind my heart make it impossible to forget. One more image comes into view: an old well house in the middle of the yard. I'm shaking. I feel as though I have fallen into my own metaphorical well, an unfathomable hole that is endless, gloomy, and overwhelmingly terrifying. As panic mounts in my mind, I close my eyes, an act that proves to be less than rewarding. I instantly visualize myself trapped deep in the well, being sucked down into thick, sticky mud that clings to my feet and makes escape impossible. The walls are lined with mud, jagged rocks, and vines with sharp thorns. I reach my hands out for help, but I draw them back instantly when they're cut by the thorns. I watch the blood drip down my arms. The walls of the well are closing in on me. I wrap my arms around myself in desperation and instinctively look toward the heavens.

There it is—a faint light.

I may be confined and confused, but I see a ray of hope.

Finding Hope and Safety

I open my eyes, and the nightmare of the well dissipates for a moment. I'm staring at the well house. I wonder, *What gives us the ability to go on in hopeless situations? More importantly, why do we lose hope in the first place?* In response to that thought, my head drops, and I look at my feet.

They are dirty, and mud has splattered all over my sandals that were once the perfect shade of white. Perfect? No, these sandals are not perfect— they are dirty, and inadequate, and imperfect—much the way I feel at this moment in time. Ironically, I have become a master at putting on the cheerful face; I am always on stage, showing those around me what they want to see, showing them how perfect I am. Truth be told, I don't feel perfect right now. I feel confined, confused, and afraid.

I have always been terrified that I would never be good enough. I've had to push, push, push myself to new heights—no matter the cost. If I had to suffer in the process, then so be it. It was a small price to pay for perfection.

But I wonder, *When we find ourselves at the bottom of our personal wells, could the light shining from above be perfection personified?* Many of us certainly act as if it were. Our minds are often wrapped around the notion that to be perfect means to be complete. We yearn to reach that light, trying desperately to claw our way to the top. Standing here now, I can almost feel the pressure of the mud beneath my fingernails. The harder I claw, scrape, and cling to the sharp muddy walls, the tighter the mud's suction tightens on my ankles. I find myself firmly anchored in place, falling short of what I believe to be the ultimate goal above. Many of us feel those walls closing in. When this happens, how can we not help but feel lonely, helpless, and insecure in the process?

I've met so many people in life who simply want to feel safe. But feeling secure and safe is such a personal notion. For some it means making steady, consistent progress toward their goals, while for others safety means something entirely different. Some live with angst in their hearts every single day of their lives. Standing here before this well house, I have to ask myself, "Am I one of them?"

Deep down, I know I have personal insecurities that entwine my faculties and tether me in place. I have always considered myself a strong woman, but there have been times in my life when these fears have horrified me with their uncanny ability to paralyze.

I AM NOT ALONE

Oh, but I am not alone. In my experiences, I have seen even the strongest of individuals crippled by fear. At the root of this fear, I believe, is the notion of perfection. The fear of striving and failing can leave us consumed with an anxiety that seems impossible to overcome. Could it be that the act of striving for perfection provides a temporary false sense of security, but ultimately ends in a case of paralyzing self-doubt?

Insecurity is like a treacherous vine at our feet, a vine that weaves its way through our lives, constricting slowly over time and suffocating us in the process. Soon we find ourselves unable to move. We trip and fall and are ultimately consumed with anxiety. Fear and insecurity have a way of infiltrating the mud-packed cracks of our psyche, ultimately breaking us apart.

In the bowels of a gloomy life experience, I often wonder where security hides. Looking up today, my gaze welcomes the depths of the trees before me. Perhaps security lies at the forest perimeter, where there is light and one can see clearly. I have spent much of my existence on the outskirts of life, searching for security only to be disappointed.

Safety, as I define it, seems elusive in the light of day. Staring into the depths of the forest today, a thrilling thought occurs to me. Perhaps safety lies hidden in the depth of trees forever protected . . . a fascinating thought. To find the comfort in life we strive for, do we plunge into the depth of the forest and battle unseen demons, or do we skirt the perimeter, a place where onlookers reside, risk is minimized, and dreams inherently die? The perimeter seems safe, yet something about the depth of the trees seems mysterious and curiously alive.

Security and Freedom

Watching the hawk surf the waves of the wind above, a thought occurs to me. *Perhaps security lies in freedom.* Could it be that when we are not being consumed by the follies of life, we are free to negotiate its highs and lows with grace? When we feel confined, on the other hand, many of us submit, and in doing so, an element of control is lost. My mind searches for examples to validate my thoughts and comes to rest on the image of my teenage son. We have been arguing regularly. He wants to be out with his friends, and my motherly instinct wants to keep him wrapped safely in a cocoon at home. Perhaps his anger and acts of defiance are a sign that he feels confined and is resisting the urge to submit—not only to my requests, but to the pressures of life in general. Of course, as parents we always have our children's safety in mind, but could it be that it is time for me to lighten up and allow him to negotiate the highs and lows in life with less interference?

My focus intensifies on the hawk: four blackbirds are mobbing her. I watch as the smaller birds dive and dart around the larger bird, obviously upset by her presence. They move progressively closer to the hawk until they are right at the tips of her wings. The hawk, attempting to make progress in the wind, endures one assault after another. She moves closer and closer to the ground until she eventually lands in a nearby tree. I watch her there, head moving from side to side, clearly taking in the situation. I am mesmerized by her statuesque presence. She stands proud and tall with her wings tucked neatly behind her. I smile. She stands calculated, wise, and silent. Her hiatus in the tree is clearly not an act of submission.

But this is not the case with my ball: it has no choice. I look down to see that the fickle grass continues to tease it back and forth as prompted by the wind. The ball's freedom is inhibited by a maze of wild blackberry vines. It is trapped, helpless, at the whim of the ruthless vines. I remember their thorny embrace from my childhood with disdain. I recall them tearing at my skin, drawing blood as they encircled my ankles, and making it difficult to move. There was no escape from the pain . . .

ESCAPE THE PAIN

I'm rocketed awake by a sharp pain on the side of my head. My legs feel heavy, and it is difficult to move them. I sense a flurry of activity around me, an urgency that is scary. I take note of my surroundings. I am lying on the ground, my legs outstretched with my arms crossed over my chest. There are sirens in the distance, and I can hear the crunch of glass under someone's shoe. There is moaning and whispering all around me. Oh God, I am scared. What has happened? Where am I?

I become acutely aware that I am actually lying in the road. My head is in the lap of my mother's friend, who is motionless and still. I sit up and look at her face. I call her name. Finally, she starts to move, grimacing and moaning as her eyes struggle to open. Blood is running from the corner of her mouth. The sun is shining brightly; it's too bright, too hot, and the heat is radiating through my body, frying my mind. But my blood runs cold. I'm confused. I'm dazed and in a state of shock.

Then I turn my head and catch sight of our Bug. The mangled mess before me no longer even looks like a car. It's just a mass of broken glass and twisted, destroyed metal. I'm frantic. I can't remember anything.

Where is my mom?

Tears are running down my face as I jump to my feet. Where *is* she? I search the faces around me. From nameless face to nameless face I go—no one will look me in the eye. They're staring down at the

continued

ground. A firm hand grasps my shoulder, and I turn to see a man in a police uniform.

"Sweetheart, you need to stay right here."

He directs me to the grass at the side of the road where my brother is. He's shaken but not hurt. My mind is screaming. I'm in a panic.

WHERE IS MY MOM?

There's a crowd of people around what once was the driver's side of the car. I catch sight of fuchsia flowers.

Her scarf . . .

I run to her through the crowd of people. The tip of the scarf is on the ground. I follow it to her neck, then her face. I stop short of touching her beautiful skin. Her face seems so calm and peaceful. Her eyes are closed, and there is no blood. She looks relaxed. Her lips are turned up at the corner of her mouth in what looks like a faint smile. She seems content, maybe even happy. Her scarf is somehow draped symmetrically around her neck in the midst of a scene of total confusion. My young mind struggles to make sense of the situation. She is lying there so peacefully—how can she be hurt? My mind is working frantically to reason its way out of this hell hole of pain. I feel pain in my head, pain in my legs, and pain in my heart.

I'm terrified as voices inside my head scream, refusing to be silent.

"She's not hurt."

"Are you sure?"

Tears stream down my face. I am trapped. I'm stuck. There's no way out. I'm in a nightmare that is not ending.

How many of us are living nightmares? Why do we let our lives get to the point where we break under pressure?

I focus again on the well house. The moss is growing, creeping steadily through the cracks in the broken boards on the sides, allowing me to peer down into the black void. I see the vines on the mud-packed walls. I bend down, pick up a stone, and toss it into the abyss, listening carefully for the impact at the bottom. I listen for what seems like an eternity. There is no sound, no bottom to hell.

I wonder how many of us have fallen into our own personal wells where we are suspended in free fall for what seems like an eternity before landing in impossible situations that have no way out. We all have been there. The bottom of that putrid place is terrifying; the walls are encrusted with the barbs of vines, sharp rocks, and cold, oozing water that chills us to our core and sucks out what is left of any warmth in our heart. The mud is our prison, where our feet are locked in place. We all likely have found ourselves trapped, terrified, and wondering, *How did I get here? What did I do to deserve this place? How will I escape?*

Set Up for Self-Sabotage

Perhaps we trick ourselves into thinking it might be easier to stay at the bottom of the well rather than to claw, grasp, and tear our way out. How many of us feel defeated, trapped, or resigned to stay in a difficult situation, no matter what the cost to our self-esteem? It is certainly a horrific form of self-abuse when we allow ourselves to rot and suffocate out of the fear of the unknown. I have been there—terrified that the long, dark, cold shaft would fill with water, leaving me with my nose barely above the surface. How many of us lose hope and ultimately go under permanently?

I have often felt trapped, stuck in a false world where I thought I should always be wanting more. After all, more is better, right? Throughout my life I have worked constantly—overworked, to be exact. Exhaustion was and continues to be for me, not a sign to slow down, but an infamous green light that tells me to go faster and faster. I have abused myself, and years of that self-inflicted abuse have kept me pinned to the floor of the prison I inadvertently constructed. In my deepest, darkest moments, voices at the bottom would whisper, "Go ahead, work a little harder and a little faster, and you will be forgiven; you will be worthy."

• • •

Needless to say, I didn't slow down. No amount of working and rushing and striving for perfection was too high. It was a small price to pay for the light at the top of the well. It was a light that promised completeness. *Perfect* and *complete* . . . I know now that from an early age, my immature mind never understood the difference between these two words. In my young mind, to be perfect meant to be complete. It did not occur to me that the very act of striving for perfection would take me down a winding road plagued with hardship and heartache. Perfection is much like the gold at the end of a rainbow; the more we chase it, the further away it gets. To confuse matters, I grew up with an alternate voice in my head suggesting that *perfection* was a dirty word meant only for braggarts and show-offs. It was a self-manufactured whisper radiating from a heart devoid of courage. I can hear it now—beckoning in the dark, leading me down a path lined with loneliness and self-doubt. It is all too clear today that both of those voices set me up for self-sabotage. Those voices were vindictive and mean and wielded a two-edged sword. One whispered, *"Perfection is a dirty word, never to be spoken."* The other hissed, *"But to be complete, you must be perfect."*

Despite kind parents and a loving family, I grew up with a battlefield in my mind. From childhood into my adult years, the notion of perfection meant being whole. To be imperfect meant failure to me, and failure was not an option. I recall night after night in podiatric medical school sitting at the desk in my dorm room studying while all my friends were out partying. I could not bear the thought of getting anything less than an "A" on a test. Success was my identity; failure meant losing a piece of my spirit, never to be seen again. Instead of admitting imperfection, I would work faster and harder—harder than anyone else. To this day, the concept of imperfection is a terrifying one, leaving me with no recourse but to strive for impossible ideals.

Pushing Harder, Feeling Worse

When I am feeling insecure, I feel as if I'm falling, plummeting into a deep, dark hole where fear means struggle, and struggle means more fear. Many of us have gone through our lives sacrificing sleep, giving up personal time, and pushing ourselves harder and harder each day. There is a price to pay later in our lives when, as a result, we find ourselves embedded in a self-made prison, unable to escape. I stand here now, front and center, and am finally being honest. I am guilty. These days I seem to be pushing harder and harder yet feeling worse and worse. The further I fall, the more I push. It is insane.

I glance back up at the tree where the hawk sits. She is now clearly agitated. With her eyes fixated on me, she shifts her weight from side to side, releases her grip on the branch, and leaps into the air. In an instant, she is airborne. To my surprise, she chooses not to climb to new heights in the crystal-blue sky, but instead is flying directly at me. Her dark eyes have got me in their sights, with her sharp beak prominent and her killer claws outstretched. She is so close that I can see the contrasting colors of her cinnamon tail feathers and her dark majestic wings. I'm forced to duck, and I feel the breeze from her powerful body brush the top of my head. She lands without a sound on the top of the well house and turns to look directly at me. I instinctively draw in a deep breath. Make no mistake, I understand that her low-flying stunt is a warning.

She stands at attention, and then, with a dramatic flap of her wings, she lets out three earth-shattering screeches, each lasting several seconds. My mind launches into action as I think, *She's talking to me!* Her calls echo through my body... *Kee-eeeee-arr! You must focus... Kee-eeeee-arr! Always pay attention... Kee-eeeee-arr! There are lessons to be learned...* I sit still, mesmerized. Not ten feet from me, she is an amazing sight.

Several minutes pass. Soon the stately bird settles down, tucks her wings neatly behind her, and stares at me intently. It's odd, and I almost feel awkward with her gaze directly upon me. I find it more comfortable to look past her than right at her, and my eyes track to the ball, still restrained by the thorny grip of the vines. It is evident that the ball cannot venture farther. It is trapped by the thorns, which have started to tear at the old red rubber. I catch sight of scratches and a hole—a hole that is allowing precious air to escape. The thought of a slow leak makes my mind rewind to thoughts of the past.

A SLOW LEAK

I can hear the slow leak of air next to me. Where *am* I? I look around to see that I am in the waiting area of an emergency room. The slow leak of air I hear is coming from a patient's oxygen tank next to me.

How did I get here?

I am confused and searching frantically for a familiar face. Everybody is staring at the floor. No one will look at me. I turn and see my grandmother. I can see that she is speaking with doctors, and it is clear that she is asking about my mother. Her presence is larger than life; it is warm, comforting, and compassionate. She scoops me into her arms. She whispers, "You will be OK. We are here." She is calm, but I sense profound sadness in her tone. I cling to her, and we both weep. Gradually I let go of her and look around. My brother is playing quietly with toy cars on the chair next to me. I watch as he systematically takes each through an obstacle course constructed of Styrofoam cups and coffee stirrers—a terrifying maze with no apparent way out.

After what seems like hours, I start wandering around the waiting room. The wandering soon turns to searching, and I innocently peer down each corridor and every hallway. I hold my breath with each turn. With every step, I encounter more faces. Friends. Loved ones. They are all here, but they won't make eye contact. Many are sitting in the waiting room, their eyes cast to the floor. Some are wiping their eyes, and others have their backs to me. Their shoulders are shaking up and down. It sounds like they are crying. But *why?* I begin to tremble . . .

WHERE IS MY MOM?

I run blindly and find myself in a hallway that is dark and cold. The walls are rough, and the paint is peeling. The floors are sticky; my sneakers make a suction sound as I walk. The light fixture above me is malfunctioning and flickering erratically in its haphazard attempt to shed light in this dark place. At the end of the hallway, I catch sight of Mommy's clothing on a gurney. Her beautiful scarf is hanging from the end. The fuchsia flowers stand out against the drab gray of the bed. My little girl's mind is struggling to make sense of everything.

They are helping her get dressed . . . surely that is what is happening . . . My mommy is OK . . . she will be back.

I turn from the gurney and come face-to-face with Grandma. Her eyes are solemn and sad as she stretches her arms toward me.

"Shelley . . ."

Her hands are shaking.

"I need to speak to you about your mom."

continued

> Suddenly I know. My mother won't be coming back. Ever.
>
> "No . . . ," I whisper as I step backward.
>
> Terror, anger, hate, and self-loathing are born in me at this moment.
>
> "No. No. *N-O-O-O-O-!*"
>
> With tears running down my face, I attempt to run past her. She catches me in her arms and holds me tight despite the fact that I am kicking and screaming.
>
> She cradles me in her arms. I feel her chest move with mine in slow sobs. She takes a deep breath.
>
> "You will stay with me now."
>
> Her arms tighten around me as we both weep. I'm acutely aware that my legs are frozen, stuck in an unspeakable muck of terror. *Please, help me; I cannot move. I cannot speak.* I'm all alone, staring at fuchsia flowers on a gray gurney.

Tears are streaming down my face as I recall the events of that day. I'm standing still with my eyes fixated on the well house. The hawk sits quietly, staring at me. Her statuesque body and piercing eyes radiate courage and strength, but it is valor I am not yet ready to accept. I feel myself back in the depths of the well. I'm trapped at the bottom, choked by recollections of the accident. *In my child's mind, the accident was my fault.* Surely I did something to deserve what happened. Surely terror and anguish don't exist for those who do everything right. So, perfection it is. I must climb . . . and if I slip, I will try again. My fists clench as I simulate clawing frantically at the mud and vines of the well wall.

I can't get out. Out of the well or what it represents—my life. I'm screaming with no one to hear. It is excruciatingly painful and lonely at rock bottom, isn't it?

How many of us have felt desolate during our lives? How many of us have given up? How many of us have been defeated in the depths of the darkness, crouching in submission?

I study the hawk before me, her claws gripping the old and rotted wood she sits upon. First my mother's death, and now my grandmother's. *Why?*

The Battle Started Inside of Me

Surely I am being punished for something I have done in the past. In light of today's situation and the accident long ago, this explanation is the only one that makes sense. What have I done to deserve this? I realize that to an outsider this rationale must seem silly and juvenile, but having lost so much, I am desperate for an explanation. Although I am standing in the sun, for all practical purposes I feel as though I am crouched in the dark at the bottom of a forgotten hole in the ground.

What happens to me is inconsequential. Does that sound familiar? Many of us go through our lives truly believing and acting as if we do not matter. Most certainly, everyone else matters—their actions, their needs are always first. When we are in that frame of mind for too long, we set ourselves up to be

> "Many of us go through our lives truly believing and acting as if we do not matter."

mistreated, smothered, or forgotten. If we don't care about ourselves, how can we expect others to care about us? I realize that in the many instances when I have been mistreated, one person and one person alone allowed it—me! I allowed it.

I have gone through life second-guessing myself over and over. I've exhibited outward confidence as an act—to hide the great internal insecurity eating me up inside. And despite having a loving, supportive family, that uncertainty continued to grow as I did. It's clear that the battle I have been fighting throughout my life started inside of me.

Sentence of Solitude

The hawk's gaze continues to fixate on me. I start to feel uneasy and insecure, as though a hole is being chiseled through my heart. Insecurity is a powerful force that penetrates our psyche, accumulates in the cracks of our being, and begins to grow. It won't let go until we are broken, bleeding, and sobbing for mercy. Right now, I am filled with all that is ugly . . . so much anger, hatred, and self-loathing.

Throughout our lives, we may encounter critics—critics who operate and hide in the shadows because we allow them to. When I was doing college and postgraduate work, I absorbed the words of others that I never told anyone about:

"You have balls." (They're uncomfortable that I am determined.)
"You will never be able to do that." (They're critical of my small stature.)
"You are too direct." (They're irritated that I speak my mind.)

• • •

But I'm not alone. For years, I've heard stories from both men and women, one more horrifying than the next, about painful situations that ended the same way—in compromise. I can recall years ago standing in the studio of a local television station on the campus of the university I attended. I was eager and proud to have written the promotional script for the news anchor. The show on air was a success, and that night I shared my triumph with friends. I had dreams of being a news anchor myself, and when I shared my passion, I was shocked at their response:

"You don't have the voice for it."

"Are you kidding me? I can't see you doing *that.*"

"There is no future in broadcasting."

"Why don't you start thinking about a career in medicine?"

What did I do in response to their criticism? Fearing failure, I compromised. I couldn't bear the idea of being anything less than perfect, so I said yes to a career in medicine and put my passion for communications on the back burner. Compromise—the ultimate Band-Aid. Looking back, I realize that I have compromised at times when I know I should not have. My attempts at perfection have left me incapable of saying no. As a result I have become burned out, depleted, and exhausted. I have exposed myself to dangers in life I am now just beginning to understand—and am only now feeling the consequences. Why did I do that? Why do I continue to do that? *To avoid feeling vulnerable. To avoid letting people see who I really am.*

I have often felt insecure, and I have known many other people who've endured feeling the same way. There is a part of me, even to this day, that whispers, "Give up, retreat to a safe place." Another part of me says, "No, come out of that place and let everyone see who you are."

My compromise to prevent people from seeing who I really am was to come out of my protected place—but to work harder and faster than everyone around me. I felt protected and secure in my safe place, yet strangely unhappy. In an attempt to justify my withdrawal from the world, I would interact with others in a defensive and suspicious manner. Stepping out of my safe place, on the other hand, was scary and oddly exhilarating. When out of my safe zone, I would proceed with caution, yet my demeanor would transition to one of hope and optimism.

Hope is what I need. What we all need. Stepping out was frightful for me but something I knew I needed to do. Day after day I would compromise; I would persuade myself to venture out of my safe place—but not without the protective shield of activity. Excessive activity kept me busy—too busy to truly interact with family, friends, or acquaintances. Although I was out and interacting in the world, I still felt isolated and alone. The more vulnerable I felt, the harder I worked. The more I added to my schedule, the better I felt about myself. I kept going no matter what the cost. But all the while my body was giving me signals of impending doom: fatigue, headaches, and sleeplessness.

Lost in the Dark

I ignored the signals. I kept going at a reckless pace, disregarding the warning signs along the way. I didn't understand, nor did I care, what I was doing to myself. I was scared to stop. Eventually I reached middle age. I'm standing here now, on this lawn, with no focus. I am lost in the dark, cold and scared. I have forgotten what it means to be me. I have crashed—bent and broken, frozen and paralyzed—under the critical gaze of one of nature's greatest creatures.

> How many of us have received this sentence of solitude and needless suffering? How many of us have endured a life of endless multitasking, a ceaseless cycle of doing things over and over, without a glimmer of success on the horizon?

It is insane, and I realize now that I have not been happy for a long time.

I'm always frantically reaching beyond myself—to people for comfort and to things for satisfaction—always without success. I have a difficult time loving myself. I often wonder how many of us feel the same way. There is a special place in our hearts for self-love. When we fail to love ourselves, a painful void in our hearts results that cannot be filled by outside people or circumstances. The affection for oneself must come from within, and it must be genuine. I have always buried myself in work in a futile attempt to fill the painful void in my heart—a void I created and only I can fill.

We all have had times when we hit the bottom of the well. But we don't deserve to stay in that godforsaken place. It has become abundantly clear to me through discussions with family, friends, and colleagues that there are three vitally important ways that we—the little girl who lost her mother, the woman who emotionally abuses herself, and you—all deserve to feel: loved, secure, and at peace.

I have to grin with the irony of it all. Today's society, overrun with violence, passive-aggressive behavior, and ever-present bullying, doesn't always allow us to have these feelings. Instead, it envelops us in fear, leaving us little strength to climb out of the mess our lives are in. But if we want to climb out, we must be strong enough to start the journey, smart enough to plan the course, and determined to get to the top once and for all.

Listen to Me

The hawk is still perched on the well house, with her strong wings tucked neatly behind her. I sense she has immense veiled strength ready to burst forth whenever she needs it. I suddenly feel an odd sense of confidence and comfort in her presence. Her eyes dart to a blackbird in a tree and then come back to rest upon me again. I think there is wisdom in her gaze, an understanding, a comprehensive knowledge that I cannot explain. As if on cue, she lets out a cry, a screech that instantly makes me focus. It's kind of crazy . . . as if she is saying, "Listen to me!"

As I gaze at the extraordinary creature before me, I realize that I can do this. I can make sense of the mess my life has become. This bird is strong, and so am I. With my mind made up, there is no one who can stop me. With that realization, I feel a surge of energy—an electricity that rushes through my veins with each heartbeat. I tear my focus from the bird and take in the scene around me with a newfound determination.

Once again I am intrigued by my childhood ball. Somehow it looks different. Curious, I tiptoe gingerly through the maze of thorny vines.

I wince as one punctures the skin on my ankle. Although I observe a drop of blood running down the side of my foot, I move forward with determination and carefully begin the process of pushing vines off the ball, one after another. I smile after the last vine drops off the cracked red rubber. The ball is free.

I pick up the liberated ball and examine it. It's battered and beaten but surprisingly full of air in spite of the slow leak. I smile as I realize that it is fully capable of bouncing! I glance at the jagged rocks at the pit of the ravine and the calm waters of the bay on the horizon. *Hmm* . . . it just needs a little help getting there. A little help is what I needed in the years following the accident. After my mother's passing, I suffered from a crazy amnesia that perplexes me to this day, and I can't recall many parts of the accident. My memories pick up when I was in kindergarten and my brother and I eventually left my grandmother's house and went to live with my father and stepmother.

• • •

I look back at the stately hawk; she seems to be guarding the well house. She shifts her weight from one foot to the other, all the while keeping her gaze on me. Then I remember my grandmother's words when she said:

"Your mind and body may be bound, but your heart is always free."

I listen in my heart to these words. Free. Yes. *Ah* . . . she saw it all along, didn't she? She saw that I was constrained and struggling to be free of my mind. Standing here under the intense gaze of this hawk, I wonder, *Where does the freedom come from?* Scenes from my childhood fly through my mind. Images of my grandmother scooping me up in a comforting bear hug ("We must be strong"), showing me how to plant a garden ("We must be smart"), and offering a quiet word of wisdom in times of need ("We must be determined"). Strength, smarts, and determination: could it be that these three qualities are essential in freeing the bonds that confine us in life?

We Are Strong

The well house stands before me with its rotted wood and weathered face. My overactive imagination returns me to the bottom of the well where I find myself constrained, claustrophobic, and terrified. I ask myself, *How do I get out?* Common sense tells me that strength is essential in crawling out of the well. I must reach deep within, find the fortitude, and lift my feet out of the muck and water. All too often we become comfortable in that muck. We sit sad and complacent, avoiding the thorny embrace of everyday life. Safety seems to be at the bottom of oblivion. To move forward in our lives, however, it is imperative that we take our focus off the grime at our feet and look at the walls, seeing the stones embedded in the dirt and reaching out to grab them. We must get the leverage and start pulling ourselves out of desperate situations. We can do this.

•••

There is strength in awareness. I feel the warmth of the sun on my arms, and it dawns on me that there is significant strength in awareness. Awareness means shedding the ignorance that shuts the door on common sense. When we're in that position, how can we not feel weak and oblivious, completely unable to pull our limbs out of the sticky confines?

I have come to realize that there's little strength in oblivion. There is, however, significant strength in awareness and understanding. That is a lesson I learned at an early age with the loss of my mother. At that time, I was a little girl who was terrified of what would happen to her, and I developed a horrendous fear of the unknown. I think everyone will agree that fear has a way of paralyzing and weakening even the strongest of spirits. But that weakness does not have to be permanent.

Shortly after the accident, my father sat down with me and explained what had happened and what caused the accident. More importantly, he explained that I would still be loved, cared for, and kept safe. With that awareness in my mind, an amazing transformation began. Much of the fear I had locked in my heart was replaced with something magnificent—an inner resolve and strength. I no longer felt paralyzed. My father gave me this gift as a child: the understanding that strength comes through awareness. I must remember to utilize that gift today to move myself out of the hole I have fallen into.

• • •

There is strength in form. Form—an interesting word. What shapes our reality? My gut instinct tells me that *we* do. That reality provides a structural foundation we depend on for strength throughout the course of our lives. We, and we alone, are responsible for how we see the world. We can either fill our reality with hope and security, or we can overwhelm it with despair and uncertainty. In my life, when I let despair and insecurity dominate me, self-hatred becomes rampant.

So many of us internalize and blame ourselves in times of strife. When we are in the depths of despair, the structure in our lives is often the only thing we have to depend on. A warm sensation fills my heart as my thoughts drift to my stepmother. Soon after I lost my mother, my father and stepmother brought us from Grandma's house to live with them. My stepmother, who I now call Mom, made a beautiful home for my brother and me, complete with warm food and kind words. When the bottom fell out of my life, the structure she provided gave me the strength to keep from sinking back into the cold, black mud. For that I will be forever grateful.

I recall that one day after coming to live with my father and step-mother, I went outside to play with the neighborhood children. On the outside, I appeared to be a happy, well-adjusted child, but inside, my child's heart cried quietly. I missed my biological mother—her smile, her smell, her presence. The children that day were playing with golf clubs. Distracted by my internal turmoil, I didn't notice one child raise his club in a swing, and *SMACK!* The club hit me hard in the mouth. I ran to the house crying, bleeding, and missing a tooth. My stepmother immediately sat me down. I remember being comforted by her calm demeanor as she washed my cuts, put ice on my bruises, and explained that the tooth fairy would soon be coming to visit me with a surprise. That day she gave me something solid to lean on and beautiful to believe in when my world seemed to be falling apart. You see, when we have structure in our lives and our foundation is solid, we become brave. It is that courage that encourages us to look within and realize that what is at our core is good and strong.

As images of my stepmother fade, memories of my grandmother come back into focus. I see her smiling, rose in hand, in the middle of her garden. I think back on several times coming into her house with my mind filled with guilt over something that had happened that week in school; maybe my grades were not high enough or someone did not like me. It didn't matter. There were days when I didn't like myself much. But then Grandma and I would work in the garden together. She would show me how to plant seeds: dig a small hole, gently place the seeds inside, cover them with dirt, and water the area. Then we would repeat the process, over and over. The task may have seemed monotonous to some, but to me it was the best therapy. There was structure to the process, a closely woven set of rules for success that when followed resulted in something exquisite: beautiful flow-ers that reached closer to the heavens with each passing day. Those moments were magical for me. They were times when I felt safe. With my heart filled with productive creativity, there was little room for guilt or self-loathing.

· · ·

There is strength in adventure. One productive idea that takes root in our minds can serve as a rung we can use to hoist ourselves out of everything that is holding us down. The possibilities are endless. Many people let exciting ideas go by the wayside for fear of failure, what others might think, or fear of the unknown. I always feel sad and weakened when I have done this. Years ago, when I left my communications major in college and went into medicine, a strange sadness came over me. I know now that my heart was objecting to the direction my life was taking while my mind reasoned its way through the process. "Medicine is a more stable career." "There is no job security in communications." My mind dominated my thoughts and won the battle. I went into medicine, and through the years I did well, but I always felt as though a piece of me was missing.

I recall the day I finally woke up. I was sitting on the floor in my bedroom, sifting through a pile of laundry. I don't know what it was about the laundry or the state of my heart at the time, but I remember that three memorable words escaped my lips: "You . . . can . . . do it!" That day I woke up and decided I was going to fill the void in my heart by pursuing my lifelong dream; it was terrifying and exhilarating at the same time. How exciting it is to nourish our inner child; it is the one true component of our being that is filled with hope, energy, and adventure.

As a little girl, I was always encouraged by my parents to read, and they made sure I had books available. After every adventure I read about, I felt stronger and more vibrant. To this day, reading sparks the flame of adventure deep in my heart. Looking at the well house, the tingle in my feet spreads to my legs in an exhilarating sensation. Studying the statuesque hawk before me, something is suddenly clear to me. To reach our goal, it is imperative that we take flight in adventure. Think about that! The sky is the limit, but to advance on this amazing adventure, we must not look to others for strength; we must reach deep and realize that the resolve to start the exhilarating climb lies within us.

Awareness, form, and adventure . . . oh yes, we must be strong.

We Are Smart

Confined to the bottom of the well of life, staring at the twigs and vines, I realize that I *may* be strong, but is that strength all I need to crawl out of the hole my life has become? Recalling failure after dreadful failure in my life, I realize that no, strength is not enough. I must be smart. That word may mean different things to different people, but standing here right now, under the intensity of the hawk's gaze, I realize that being smart means being prepared, confident, and resourceful.

Oh yes . . . being smart means being prepared. Peering into the black depths of the well, I visualize myself stuck in the black mud. I have the strength to pull myself out, but I realize that the journey to the top is not an easy one. I realize that exhaustion will become a reality if my foothold on the slippery vines and rocks is not planned appropriately.

CLIMB UP AND OUT

I will be the first to admit that I have personally suffered the consequences of acting without thinking. Acting without thinking is common. I've done it many times in my life, but you know what? I know better. Before I do it this time, I will take a look at the entire picture before climbing through the vines to my goal. Only after the course is strategically mapped out will I embark on the journey to the top: one foothold, one firm grasp after another. I will climb! Climb up and out.

Growing up, I recall watching my father day after day in his tool shop. My father was and is my hero. He could fix anything. What intrigued me was his attention to detail. He would lay out each tool. The plan was clearly set before embarking on a project. It was ingrained in me as a child that success on any journey in life lies in part on the shoulders of solid preparation. I recall summer after summer camping with my parents. Proper preparation played a major role in the success of our trips. I would watch my father's steady hand as he checked the tire pressure on the trailer's wheels. My stepmom would diligently plan our daily menu, carefully choosing foods that were fun and tasty. Translating that to my life, my journey, it is clear to me that preparation is a prerequisite to success.

Learning this valuable lesson from my parents, I was always prepared in school, in college, and in my career as a podiatrist, but there are certain things that an eager heart finds difficult to prepare for—hurtful people, for instance. People who have no other motive but to demean and degrade. My mind suddenly drifts back to a sunny day in middle school. I am running outside to play soccer. Then, at the edge of the field, I see the crowd of kids shouting. I approach the group in my memory, and I realize that the crowd is shouting at a girl sitting on a bench with her head hung low.

"Smelly Shelley." (Her name was the same as mine.)

"Why don't you cover your head with a paper bag?"

"No one likes you. Go play by yourself."

As I reached out to pull on the arm of one of the instigators, the crowd dispersed, leaving us alone together. I sat with her that day and attempted to console her, but her bruised heart refused to let me close. The hair on my arms stands on end today remembering that scene. It was my first encounter with bullying; little did I know that this experience put me on high alert. To this day, any time I witness demeaning behavior, I speak out against the perpetrator with ferocious tenacity.

Watching Shelley go through that humiliation in a strange way prepared me for the narcissistic, abusive behavior I would encounter later in life.

BE PREPARED FOR THE BULLIES

That experience sent a strong message to me. Good, kind, and compassionate individuals in this world must be prepared for people who cross their paths who are mean and vindictive, those who are not interested in the health and well-being of others. Some people will want to see us fail; they won't have our best interest at heart. How do we prepare? We fill our battle holsters with the antidotes to hateful behavior.

- When we are confronted with hate, we react with kindness.

- When we are confronted with jealousy, we react with compassion.

- When we are confronted with anger, we react with love.

Ironically, in some instances, *we* are those hateful people. Oh yes, we are. I have been there myself more times than I want to admit. We're jealous of those around us and fearful of their success. Why? We're afraid that we won't succeed in life and suspicious of others who might. When we have clear-cut goals and are confident in the direction our life is taking, we become empowered and less obsessed with what others are doing. On the other hand, if we are not prepared with a well-thought-out plan, thoughts of inadequacy suffocate the life out of all we hold dear. Although it is impossible to predict what life has in store for us, knowing what we want in our lives and laying out a tentative plan for moving forward minimizes the unknown and loosens the vines of fear.

Being smart means being confident. I have found over the years that confidence seems to come after performing a task repetitively until success ensues. I chuckle . . . I have been known to fail 100 times and succeed on the 101st attempt. Oh yes, repetition has been good to me. I recall sitting in the cadaver lab in medical school practicing a suture technique called the horizonal mattress. The horizontal mattress suture technique, when done properly, leaves the skin edges smooth and flush, which in a living human provides for adequate healing. That day, I attempted over and over to perfect this technique. I sat there for hours. No success. The skin would bunch up on one side or the other; it wasn't working for me. So frustrating! After numerous attempts, I sat back and looked around me. The instructor was demonstrating the suture technique on the table next to me. I watched. I learned. *Ah*, the light bulb went on! My spacing was not right. I took what I had learned, sat back down, and after a few more attempts, perfected the stitch. I beamed with confidence that day. With practice comes confidence.

If we are staring up at those jagged walls that confine us, strength may help us find our footing, but confidence is what prompts us to grasp the vines above us and pull ourselves up so we can climb those walls. Confidence is what keeps us moving when we slip on our journey, always prompting us to find another way. Taking a deep breath, I recall my residency director's words: "A good surgeon is not one who does the procedure perfectly; a good surgeon is one that does the procedure over and over again and knows what to do when things go wrong."

> **"Confidence is what keeps us moving when we slip on our journey, always prompting us to find another way."**

That's a liberating comment. Even when we do things perfectly, things go wrong in life. But what we need to remember is that our actions do not have to be perfect. Our results in life do not have to be perfect. We must not blame ourselves if things go wrong. If only we had a handbook telling us what to do and not to do in certain situations, right? I smile as I think of my oldest son. I sure could have used a parenting handbook last week. It was a rainy night in South Florida, and I took my daughter and her friends to the movies. I left my oldest son, his friend, and my youngest son at home. When I arrived at the movies, I got a frantic call from my youngest son.

"Mom, Trevor has taken your car!"

Taken my car? I was confused. He was fifteen and didn't even have a learner's permit. Surely this could not be the truth.

"Are you sure?"

"Yes, Mom, I'm sure. I will send you a picture."

Sure enough, the picture my son texted me showed my oldest son and his friend in my brand-new car. They had waited until I left, found the key, and took it for a ride to "pick up friends." Driving home that night, I was dazed, confused, and angry. Surely my son knew that this was the wrong thing to do. My mind began its attack on my psyche.

It's because you haven't been a good mom.

You are not spending enough quality time with him.

You shouldn't have left him alone.

One thought, one assault after another, until I pulled into the driveway. My son had arrived home with my car. I sat in the driveway for a moment and took a deep breath. As my mind began to quiet, I could hear my heart whisper:

You are a good mom.

You do spend enough time with him.

He is old enough to be home alone. Tonight he made a mistake.

I walked calmly into the house that night. As I explained to my son the consequences of his actions, I realized something important. There are times in our lives when things go wrong even when we have done what we know in our hearts to be right. My son took the car, but it wasn't because I was a terrible mom. In times of strife, we must find the strength to move forward, learn from what has happened, and go on. There are times in life when our internal foundation is less than sure.

If our footing slips, we must simply find another foothold and continue on. No matter what we have done in life, I firmly believe that we most certainly do the best we can with what we have available physically and emotionally at that particular moment in time. We do the best we can with what we are presented. Forgiving ourselves and

> **"We do the best we can with what we are presented."**

others is essential. To get to the top, we must work smart, shed the blame, feel the confidence, and continue on our journey to our goal.

Being smart means being resourceful. I exhale and visualize myself climbing the muddy walls of the well, climbing out of the confines that suffocate me. I find and grab vine after vine. Looking up in the direction of the light, I feel mud and water droplets sting my face. I take one foothold after another and hoist myself up. It occurs to me that success in life for many is about accessing, trusting, and utilizing our inborn instincts, those internal aptitudes that have only our best interest at heart. These instincts are the ultimate resource, and if listened to, keep us safe from the thorns of life. They help us move in a positive direction; as we move upward toward our goal, we grow.

• • •

My gaze moves beyond the well house, and I catch sight of a long, lanky stem with a brilliant yellow sphere at the top. It is a sunflower. The sunflower marks the spot where my grandmother used to bury her table scraps from dinner. I watched year after year as that area sprouted and gave birth to small apple tree seedlings, potato vines, carrots, and much more. These scraps might have looked like garbage to all of us, but not to Mother Nature—and not to my grandmother. The plants grew in that location without question or hesitation, recycled and resourceful as nature intended. A plant's instincts are true. Unlike a human being, a tree doesn't analyze how it grows; it just does. We must trust that ever-important force that resides within all of us. We must hold on tight and pull ourselves up and grow in the process.

Prepared, confident, and resourceful . . . Oh yes, we must be smart.

We Are Determined

I sigh . . . if we are climbing up the grimy walls of life and our goal is in sight at the top, strength helps us move forward and being smart helps us plan, but what happens if we get halfway up and become tired? What if we're exhausted and can't move another inch?

There we are, in the frustrating position of knowing where we need to go and how we need to get there but stopping short after running out of physical or emotional stamina. I have been at that point. When I was a surgical resident, I was at the end of a rotation in the hospital and hadn't slept in forty-eight hours. After a hectic night of stitching up wounds in the emergency room, starting IVs on the floor, and attending to patients, I was exhausted. No, I was frozen—so tired and hungry I couldn't take another step. I felt like giving up. Out of desperation, I slipped into a utility closet; I sat on a stool in the dark, closed my eyes, and let my emotions close in around me. I recall thinking, *If I leave now, all my hard work will be for nothing.* At that very moment, images of my friends, colleagues, and family engulfed me like a warm cocoon. They were cheering for me from the light at the end of the tunnel. In the dark that night, I found the strength to go on.

"I will not give up."

"I will continue to move forward."

"I will not be defeated."

With that, I got up off of the stool, opened the closet door, and finished my rotation.

It is a terrifying feeling to be hanging in limbo—afraid to fall back but too exhausted to move forward. When that happens, it is imperative that we look around, take note of others who have succeeded, and analyze their actions. They may be tired, but they have one desirable trait that keeps them climbing faster and higher than the rest: they have determination. They are determined to overcome obstacles, complete the journey, and pursue their true purpose with passion and conviction.

Being determined means overcoming obstacles. As we make progress toward our goals, obstacles have an uncanny knack of getting in the way. I certainly have had problems interrupt my progress in life—overwhelming schedules, financial burdens, and family obligations, to name a few. I know that I am not alone.

Images of two women I have encountered in my life come to mind. Both went through brutal divorces, and both were equally devastated at the time. Interestingly, each dealt with the aftermath of their divorce differently. One woman went on to get her teaching degree and is living a life full of love and adventure. She approaches each day with optimism. The second woman is a shell of her former self. She spends her days reliving the divorce, and to this day she's plagued with anger, hatred, and fear. The difference between the two women is remarkable. It has often puzzled me how many people I know who have been stopped suddenly by the smallest obstacle and were never able to move upward again; still others encounter obstacles, stop momentarily, and then find a way around, through, or over the problem. What makes the difference? It's plain and simple: mental fortitude.

You see, we all have a choice. The vines in the well of life can either stop us or empower us to move past them. Which will it be? Perhaps an obstacle is more likely to stop us if we obsess over the daunting distance we need to climb. When we focus on what is left of our journey, it is easy to run out of that all-important energy as our minds trick us into thinking we can't possibly move further. We have to look back to see how far we have come. Many of us could use that reassuring pat on the back, the validation that comes from acknowledging how much we have accomplished in our lives. A simple affirmation, like an unseen cheerleader, is often enough to inflate our energy levels and allow us to move forward despite the barriers. It is all too clear. If we are to reach our goals, we must remain determined through the entire process, regardless of the obstacles. We can't merely *think* we will make it: we have to *know* that we will and keep climbing at all costs ...

Being determined means completing the journey. I recall a pivotal moment in my life when I left the safety of a career that was secure and comfortable. I was a physician; I had completed four years of undergraduate training, four years of podiatric medical schooling, and a surgical residency. When I graduated, I joined a thriving practice and built a patient base and reputation of which I was proud. The problem was that I was comfortable—too comfortable. There was no excitement in my days. I stumbled through the years, always feeling like a piece of me was missing. At that time in my life, I found myself stagnant and unhappy, hanging on the muddy wall of life, frozen in place.

And then it happened. On the brink of divorce, I sat defeated on my bedroom floor, tears streaming down my face, trying to sort out the mess my life had become. I had a decision to make: I could stay frozen and seemingly safe on the sides of the wall, or I could venture out, leave what was lucrative, take a risk, and follow the path I intuitively knew to be true for me. Leaving behind that which is comfortable is scary, but it's exhilarating as well. Despite the naysayers and criticism, I made the decision to pull myself up into an unknown yet exciting frontier. Many have asked why I decided to venture forward into unknown territory, and they are often surprised at my one-word answer.

Defeatism.

Defeatism surrounded me everywhere. In the office. At home. In the supermarket. Even today, everywhere I go, it is there. I often accepted defeat without question. Why? *Because I carry it with me.* Defeatism is in my mind. Many of us have a cruel voice that dominates us and is intolerant of rational thought. That voice is the one that tells us that we are nothing, that we don't matter. Its opinion is strong and difficult to ignore. To get to the top, to complete the journey, we must silence that voice, pluck it out of our minds, and let it fall to the depths of oblivion at the bottom of the cold, dark well where

> **"Many of us have a cruel voice that dominates and is intolerant of rational thought. That voice is the one that tells us that we are nothing, that we don't matter."**

it belongs. Only then can we hear the one voice that radiates truth and justice—a higher voice that has learned from a lifetime of turmoil. It whispers, "You are good, you are worthy; stop the insanity!" We must decide for ourselves to stop the insanity so defeatism will take its grip off our spirit and let us crawl to freedom.

Being determined means pursuing our true purpose with passion and conviction. There is always a light at the top of the well. At the top is something magnificent and beautiful: our true purpose lies there. Visualize that light above. When you get there, what good will you do? Who will you help? What difference will you make?

• • •

I glance at Grandma's house and see myself as a little girl cuddling with her on a porch chair. Such warm, vivid memories I have of her on that porch! I close my eyes and my imagination takes over. I am walking down the pathway leading to the porch. The walkway is lined with purple and pink flowers that sway in the breeze. The porch chair is weathered with small cracks. Yes, I see them now: my initials carved into the armrest. I smell the familiar scent of lavender and know without looking up that Grandma is there, sitting patiently waiting for me to jump into her lap and tell her about my day.

The birds are singing a sweet melody as I remember how her strong arms wrapped around me in a reassuring embrace. As the breeze brushes across my face, I think, *Yes, we are all placed on this earth to bring two things to individuals who have lost their way: love and light—the essence of the soul.* When we're in the dark and the cold, we should be acutely aware of the power that shines from above. We've talked about the light at the top of the well. That light is the love and light of many of those in our lives who wish us well, who shine light on our path, who make each successive foothold and handhold easier than the last. We are never truly alone.

We are surrounded by an energy that comforts and lifts us to new heights. Look for it. Feel it and move on. Push forward with determination—a determination fueled by guts, grit, and stamina. I have it in me. We all have it in us. We

"We are never truly alone."

just need to feel it and realize its power. Only then are we able to move forward in our lives with purpose. This energy is a positive force that cannot be stopped.

I recall my daughter's first steps as a toddler. She would crawl over to the couch, pull herself up, steady herself, and then let go. I would watch with anticipation as she would take one shaky yet incredibly determined step—and then fall. Did she give up? Oh no, not my girl! She would crawl back to the

"We have to shed the charade once and for all and pursue what we are meant to do."

couch and start the process all over again. You could see it in her eyes: a strong, unshakable purpose that would not be swayed by temporary obstacles. As we continue to climb skyward, we must be honest with ourselves and really analyze what we want in life. We have to shed the charade once and for all and pursue what we are meant to do.

Feel the grit beneath your fingernails and dig in deeper. It is time.

Time to get to the top; the grass at the edge of the well is within sight. You can see it now: Small purple flowers are your welcome. It is time to lose the bonds and climb out once and for all. It's especially important that we remain driven and committed even after we get to the top, because that is where the real work begins. At the top we have to let go of our ego and let it fall . . . fall . . . fall until it is forever silenced in the stagnant mud below. We must do what it takes to heal our minds, assist others to do the same, and continue on a journey that quite literally never ends.

Overcoming obstacles, completing the journey, and pursuing our talents . . . and yes, we must be determined.

The Bonds of Love and Light

My thoughts trail away as I turn again to the hawk perched proudly on the well house. I see her talons tighten in the rotted wood of the structure. It is as if she is relieved.

"*Kee-eeeee-aar!*"

I smile. I have made it out of my metaphorical well. Could this be a screech of approval? She slowly expands her long brown wings in a three-foot-wide display. I find myself holding my breath. She is so beautiful! With one graceful leap she is in the air and climbing to new heights toward the light of the sun. I watch, captivated. She is truly a free spirit, defying gravity to climb to new heights. My grandmother was right: Nature does have the answers. Reflecting on her words today has helped me. I, too, feel free for the first time in my life.

Dropping my gaze in response to the brightness of the sun, I once again find myself fixated on my childhood ball. Liberated by my newly realized freedom, my heart fills with an odd compassion for the inanimate object. I step forward, gingerly pushing the last of the vines off the old faded rubber. I cradle it in my hands. I can see now that the ball, broken out of its thorny prison, has cracked rubber, but the cracks have not penetrated the interior. I sense that there are bonds beyond what I can see that hold the ball together despite its damaged, broken exterior. These bonds keep the interior safe from harm, leaving the ball fully capable of bouncing when the need arises. As human beings, we are much the same. Our exterior may be cracked, but invisible bonds exist that keep our intimate interior safe from harm. When we feel trapped by impossible circumstances, narcissistic people, and our own self-ridicule, these bonds are what lend us the *strength, smarts, and determination* to climb out of impossible situations. We all have them within us.

I'm thinking about the day I lost my mother in the accident, and it occurs to me that rubber is to a ball what metal is to a car. This ball's rubber may be cracked, yet it still holds and protects the precious air within. Some of the air has been released, free to float and join the waves of wind above. In a similar fashion, our car's exterior was cracked, scratched, dented, and even crumpled; but the metal was made with the ability to bend and flex with forces applied. That flexibility protected those of us who survived.

Some who have fulfilled their destiny are released to the cosmos and serve as the source of love and light for all of us on earth. After today, I firmly believe that my mother was not lost the day of that accident. Through energy, there are bonds that exist in nature that can never be broken, through which we will all be forever connected. Loved ones will eternally blanket us in love, acceptance, and trust, providing us with a safe interior of kindness, solitude, and healing. The bodies of those loved ones may be gone, but we will forever be connected by the bonds of love and light.

With a newfound energy, I lower the ball below my waist and then fling it high into the air, high over the rocks and out into the smooth, tranquil waters of the bay. It travels far above danger and off into adventure, a direction in which many would like to go. We all want to be in a place of safety and security. It is there that our minds and bodies can bounce back from anything.

I am reminded once more of my grandmother's words: "Your mind and body may be bound, but your heart is always free."

She was trying to tell me that when we exist at the bottom of the well of life, our minds are at war. The sticky black mud binds our bodies in a state of confusion that at times may seem impossible to overcome. Every time we attempt to pull ourselves out, the mud pulls back with equal vigor, and darkness and silence keep us entwined in fear. Perhaps the battlefields in our lives exist because of resistance. We face so much resistance in everyday life: my boss isn't happy with my work, a friend is upset with the way I spoke to her, or a family member says I didn't visit enough. Resistance leads to guilt, which leads to the mind endlessly searching for justification and solutions. It's an insane cycle that results in a plummeting sense of self-worth.

The blackbirds that heckled the hawk earlier are squabbling, and I watch as they quarrel among themselves. The bickering soon fades into silence. They seem to squabble and forget. Forgiving and forgetting seems to be an easy task, but most people I know don't do it. As they ruminate, resistance becomes the ultimate obstacle, one that must be overcome. Resistance is a wake-up call. We must wake up and realize that our hearts are calling, summoning our minds to fall into alignment. It is the way nature intended it to be.

If we find our days cold and dark at the bottom of life's well, perhaps it is a sign that resistance is preventing our hearts and minds from working together. There is no balance. The inevitable result is turmoil: With the heart and mind at odds, the mind goes to battle. It's a process that ultimately takes its toll on our bodies, often resulting in sickness and fatigue. When we feel confined and trapped in circumstances dictated by forces in life that seem beyond our control, the mind cannot help but dominate. It runs away with our thoughts and holds our heart hostage. I wonder, *What battle am I fighting right now? Do I feel resistance in my mind? How would it feel if my heart were truly free?*

I watch the hawk tilt back and forth in the wind overhead. But then I am struck by a sharp contradiction: we should *not* follow our hearts. We should *not* follow our minds. We must aim for something higher.

Balance, Not Perfection

We must aim for balance. Balance, not perfection, is the light at the top of the well and is only achieved when the heart and the mind are in alignment. The ability to bounce and not break under the perils of daily life lies in balance. When our lives are balanced, we are better able to cherish the time we have on this earth and respect the situations into which we have been put. I have learned from the past that life is fragile and can crack in an instant. We need to take the time each day to fully appreciate its significance. We are here for a reason. Perhaps a different reason for each of us—but a reason nonetheless.

And once we use our strength, smarts, and determination to crawl out of the prison, we must not become too comfortable. As I said earlier, we have to have a plan to grow, or our forward progression will be indefinitely stunted and we'll lose our sense of personal safety. When we are in a state of imbalance, it is often easy to lose sight of who we are as individuals. We become lost in the depths of the darkness, a place where the mud keeps our legs anchored and the vines tear at our flesh.

I take a deep breath and look around. As it stands right now, my life is not in balance. I struggle daily to maintain a business, to be an attentive mother and a caring wife. At the end of most days, I sit exhausted on the edge of my bed asking the question, "What about me?" It has been this way for years, and I have become accustomed to it. I have spent my days in a whirlwind of activity with my internal critic telling me what I have to do in the name of perfection. I am, ironically, comfortable but certainly not content with the way my life has unfolded. There is so much that I want to do!

I wonder how many out there feel the same way. We must break free of the bonds we place on ourselves; we must turn from critic to cheerleader. These shackles restraining us are not fair and rob us of our freedom. They are not to be tolerated. The freedom to truly experience the world in its wonder and excitement is something we owe ourselves. We *do* matter. A strong sense of personal security is a treasure that is found when the vines of confinement are finally eliminated. Do you hear me?

> **"There is so much that I want to do!"**

• • •

I stand here today as a woman, but there is still a part of that scared little girl inside me. It's a small piece that has had a big influence in my life over the years. As I'm acknowledging this fact, something important occurs to me: there will always be vines in life that encircle our limbs and threaten to strangle the life out of us. But they do not have to tighten. Like my ball—the cracks in life happen, but they do not have to deepen to the point where we suffer forever. We all possess the innate ability to venture beyond the bonds that confine us. We owe it to ourselves to break free.

You see, my grandmother knew that I had lost sight of who I was. Looking back now, remembering her kind words and compassionate gestures, she knew I was living a separate life. I was surrounded daily by busy people and overwhelming activity, but I felt curiously alone— alone with a mind and heart out of balance, bound by resistance and frozen in fear. She knew my secret. The wells we create in our lives have walls, real walls that confine. We all have them. But there is something to remember: what we may not realize is that those walls share borders . . . mine with yours, yours with mine.

Our prisons do share walls. Ironically, we are attracted to what binds us. As a society we seem riveted to the television, radio, and internet, where we are assaulted by ignorance, bigotry, and egoism. Each of these factors sticks to us, vine after vine, confining us in a cold, dark prison. But it doesn't have to be that way. We must look to nature. Nature finds ways to stay connected and still remain free. We can live in symbiosis, not bondage.

I watch as a butterfly elegantly lands on a flower near me. As it works diligently on the flower, the concept of symbiosis in life becomes abundantly clear. The flower needs the butterfly as the butterfly needs the flower. The butterfly helps to spread the seed of the flower, and the butterfly in turn is nourished by the flower's abundant supply of nectar. It is important to note that each is an energy being, and the actions of one do not hinder the forward progression of the next. They exist to assist one another. We simply must remember that we are all energy beings, each with a uniquely positive gift that must be utilized. In the broad scheme of life, we exist to spread positive energy from being to being and bathe all on our journey in the love that radiates from within.

It Was Not My Fault

What puts the cracks in our psyche over time? Our attempts at perfection. Is perfection possible? It is entirely clear to me that we are not put on this earth to be loved because we are perfect. We are here to be loved for our imperfections. Our imperfections make us who we are. We are individuals who are perfectly imperfect. That's such a beautiful thing. Ironic, isn't it? I have been striving for something my entire life that already exists.

Grandma's bottom-line message to me today is all too clear. And my bottom-line message to all of you is the same: it was not my fault. The accident, the hospital, and my mother's death. All of it.

IT WAS NOT MY FAULT.

It's so liberating to say. I sigh as I feel the weight lift off my heart. "It's not my fault." Yet I have spent a lifetime punishing myself and trying to reach society's definition of perfection. I realize now that all my activity was merely a cover for the insecurity and fear in my heart. The overloaded schedule and overworked mind served as a personal sentence for a crime I did not commit. My immature mind took a difficult situation and internalized it into blame. It was the only way to make sense of a terrifying ordeal.

Many of us carry past trauma into adulthood, leaving years of self-induced abuse in its path. Insane! It is obvious to me today that we must silence those hateful words in our heads. All is as it is meant to be. There is no such thing as perfection as the material world sees it. Perfection is what we truly see in the moment—the bay, the trees, the beautiful hawk. We are part of that reality—our well walls are aligned. We are put on this earth to assist one another,

"All is as it is meant to be."

and that is perfection at its best. We are perfect as we are, and we cannot under any circumstances feel like we are anything less than that. Those voices in my head that tell me that I am nothing are terrifying, but they are wrong. Do you hear me? *They are wrong.* Do not listen to them. When we hear their evil whisper, we must think of what brings us joy, what makes our hearts sing.

And Do It Now!

Don't waste time. Life is not about struggle and misery. It is not about constant sacrifice. Thinking that way will not liberate us from our thorny confines. Only *we* can shed what binds us. Climb to freedom!

As my mind drifts back to reality, I look to the sky. I again catch sight of the hawk, now gliding effortlessly through the air. She is my guardian angel, watching over me—energy in motion, nothing lost, and nothing gained. Simply perfect—perfection in flight. She negotiates the wind without a care, clearly encountering *no resistance*. Her mind, body, and spirit are in sync. It's time for me to relax now, with a heart and a mind that are in balance.

• • •

My eyes return to the waves of the bay where my childhood ball floats freely, bobbing up and down in the cool, dark water. It's no longer restricted and spins joyfully with each passing wave. Its rubber is glistening in the sun. Today I think of the obstacles it has endured—the harsh sun, the rain, the vines, the rocks, and the cracks in its outer hull. Despite them all, it is now free to float into a new adventure.

For the first time in my life, I feel like I have taken a direct path through the darkness and arrived in the light. Up until now, I have been walking around with deep, disturbing feelings, trying to pretend they didn't exist. I will be the first to admit that it is so much more difficult to deal with problems when we are constrained in a prison we construct. Once we shed the shackles of blame, we are free to climb out of the torment our lives sometimes become. Perhaps it is faster and easier than we think. We must free ourselves from the obsession of what *could be* and focus instead on what *is*. We must first negotiate the battlefield in our minds, and then we must conquer fear. Conquer fear, not brush it under the carpet and hope that it will go away. We must find the strength to persevere and throw off the shackles that hold us in bondage. We must size up our obstacles and summon the ingenuity and intelligence to move past them. Most importantly, it is imperative that we reach deep and call upon our inner determination—an innate drive that calls on us to make a positive difference in the lives of all living creatures.

We must live lives that are free. Like the hawk soaring freely above me, we must live that life in flight. Like the ball, we must float freely and not resist when life pushes in the direction of our next journey. We are perfectly imperfect, just as we are meant to be. We must open our ears and listen, open our hearts, and feel the truth. I catch sight of the beer can in the bushes—another piece in this scene that has taken me back to the past and into the present again. I smile. Blue metal with white writing like the sky and clouds above my head. It will be good to finally let my mind rest.

You know . . . I think I could go for a nice cold beer right now.

With her words, in her silent way, my grandmother was trying to tell me that when we try too hard, we set ourselves up for failure. Although it is not always easy, we need to let go and let life happen. Holding on too tightly is a waste of time. I have never begged for anything in my life, but to all of the desperate men, overburdened women, and insecure children out there, I am begging you now. We must vow to never sell ourselves short. We all deserve to feel loved, not persecuted; peaceful, not overwhelmed; secure, not fearful.

There will always be loss, sadness, violence, bullying, and missteps in life. And taking chances to overcome these things means making changes and learning lessons.

That little girl who lost her mother so long ago has learned many lessons. She has dedicated her life to assisting others in developing the strength, smarts, and determination to make a difference. A funny thing happens when we turn our personal pain into a positive life lesson for others. The dark place deep in our minds is lit by a spark that warms the soul. The world does not establish our value. Our worth is instilled in us from the very beginning. It is the one true thing that needs no defense. All of us should be beaming with pride. We are powerful. That power allows us to break free of the bonds that restrain, and it allows us to turn those personal battlefields into freedom fields. We can do this. After all, we *are* perfect—perfectly imperfect as human beings are meant to be.

Part Five

PEACE, LOVE, AND LIGHT

"Saying goodbye doesn't mean anything. It's
the time we spent together that matters . . ."

—Trey Parker

She Is Not Gone

Standing in the yard now, I slip off my sandals and immediately feel the cool, soft grass brush against my feet. I turn and glance up the hill to the driveway. My grandmother's funeral awakened the frightened little girl in me. I descended the hill as a despondent child who lost her mother years ago; the loneliness, panic, and guilt resurfaced with a vengeance, threatening to never go away.

We have all suffered through miserable times in our lives. There may be moments when we feel like a ball bouncing endlessly through the highs and lows of everyday life. While the highs can be exhilarating, the lows can be terrifying. As I walk away from the embankment's edge today, I study my dirty feet as they glide through green blades of grass. One thing is certain: we can't stop drama from showing up in our lives, but we can control how we react to it. I am convinced that we are resilient; we can break a heart, break a nail, or break a glass, but our souls will be forever resilient. How liberating . . .

My reflection today has been painful yet curiously therapeutic. My inner child has been taken on a journey, a journey through nature's metaphors. Oh yes, Grandma was right: nature does have the answers. The struggling duck reminded me of the patient in the office; his obnoxious behavior exemplified the ultimate bully and underscored the fact that we must always have a solid foundation to deal with the stress in life—or the bully will win. The ostracized goose brought back memories of my son and the baby goat, reminding me that perceived rejection does not have to result in loneliness and isolation. When we give from a heart that is true and genuine, rejection turns to loving acceptance. We are all worthy of love, and we should never forget that. The stately hawk served as an all-important reminder of my mother's death, shedding light on the fact that the pursuit of perfection does not drive away the guilt and shame we can feel. Forgiveness—of ourselves—must come from within.

Most importantly, this day has taught me that our personal foundations must be built on solid ground for us to have any chance of surviving the pain and loss that can come our way. Sometimes we do have good personal foundations, but the ups and downs of living make us forget that we do. And every solid foundation lasts and endures because we put in the faith and hard work to develop meaningful relationships. We must be willing to let down barriers and allow others close to what we hold sacred. When we forgive, we dissolve barriers that allow those who care for us close once again.

I walk back to the garden today and stand at its center. I feel relaxed now, yet oddly exhilarated. What a difference a little quiet time has made. My senses are alive; an electricity is flowing through my veins unlike anything I have felt before. I feel the sun warm me and radiate through my body, bursting from within. I feel like I am glowing. The autumn air is cool and crisp, promising a new season full of adventure. A mockingbird is singing in the apple tree next to me with such a sweet, inviting sound. The scene before me is now warm and inviting, unlike the cold, gloomy landscape I encountered upon first arriving. I take a breath of fresh air and wonder: *Why the difference?* My heart whispers, *You have peace in your mind, love in your heart, and light in your soul.*

I realize now that the loneliness, panic, solitude, and guilt I have felt will not go away until it has taught me what I need to know. I know now that what holds me together is not people or circumstances. What holds me together is the fiber of my being. It is what radiates from my soul. It is in me, and it is in all of us. But we must listen—listen to others, listen to nature, and most importantly, listen to ourselves. Intuition is worth a thousand words; it is a heartfelt whisper that tells us that we have purpose. I am on a mission to tell my story to minimize suffering for those in whom resides an inner child screaming to be heard. For many of us, that voice has been silenced for far too long. Acknowledging our scars helps us understand the lessons to be learned; that is how true healing begins.

A thought that I cannot ignore pops into my head: *Grandma is not gone.* She will never be gone. As the wind touches my hair and moves wisps of it across my face, I realize that she will always be here with me. A friend, a confidante, a playmate, a cook, a support system. She was my grandmother.

Standing in the middle of this magnificent garden today, I feel the energy that surrounds me. I catch sight of a single flower standing proudly in the middle of the garden. It is not sad and wilting—oh no, it stands proud, refreshed by the recent rain. It is vibrant. Just look at it! A gorgeous full rose, glistening in the sun and nourished by the soil. That flower is exactly what I remember from my childhood. The sweet smell brings back beautiful memories that blanket me in comfort and security.

Until the day she died, my grandmother was insistent that life's previous memories be written down. *This* is my life's log.

Oh yes, Grandma, I am writing!

My fingers are flying over the keys, guided by the love in my heart, the light in my mind, and the peace in my spirit. Writing life's experiences down makes them real. I feel connected and so close to her. A beautiful feeling.

. • .

I turn and walk up the driveway. I descended this hill as an apprehensive child and now ascend as a confident woman—a woman who has learned and will continue to learn many life lessons. As my feet scuff the pebbles at the top of the hill, I turn to take in the beauty of my grandmother's property.

Dear reader, picture this canvas:

The apple tree stands to my right, tall and stately, branches dancing elegantly in the wind. When we see an apple tree, let it be a reminder to live a balanced life, a reminder to take a good look at our priorities and in some cases slow down. We must remember that rigidity weakens the spirit; flexibility is strength. Standing firm on a strong foundation is essential; its strength allows us to truly listen when our spirit warns of imbalance.

The beautiful bay in front of me flows into the horizon. It's a backdrop that calms the spirit. When we see a large expanse of water, may that remind us of the concept of control. Constructing barriers in life often lends a sense of control, but it can ultimately lead to isolation and loneliness. Only *you* control you. We have to stop fighting over what we have little control over. When we stop fighting, there is little need for barriers.

My grandma's garden stands proudly to the left, a wild array of flowers and greenery—perfectly imperfect. When we see a garden, may it remind us all that we are unique. Each of us possesses essential gifts, but collectively we are one. We must stop chasing the concept of perfection. Perfection is often what we are not, and we waste precious time searching for it. Look within and know that perfection quite simply lies in what *is*—right here, right now. It's what resides within, the spark in our soul that burns brightly, untouched by the material world. It is the good that resides deep at the core of our being.

Are we listening? Nature is whispering. It is telling us that we are guided by a force that radiates from within, an energy that softens pain and promotes healing. Oh yes, feel the energy. We are all resilient, powerful, and adventurous beings. It is truly a glorious world. Instead of seeing death, pain, and suffering, I see a beautiful butterfly before me right now. I watch as it lands gracefully on a flower. From here on out, I will make changes. When I am tired, I will rest. When I feel defeated, I will rejuvenate. When I am lonely, I will reach within. I realize that my grandmother's words are forever etched into my memories—so fortunate and magical for me. As she was known to say:

"Life is life. What will be will be. How we handle the ups and downs of life is our choice. What do we choose?"

Will we break?

Or will we bounce?

Oh, there is no question for me. *I will bounce!* I will not let myself become brittle with neglect. I will nurture myself and those around me by basking in the glory of love, light, and peace. Only then are we fully capable of bouncing back when the storms in life push through.

My eyes close slowly, and I draw in a deep breath through my nose. My heart rate slows to a calm rhythm as my mind relaxes. Waves of brilliant color become visible through my closed eyelids. I observe in fascination as the colors consolidate and take form. Take shape—into what? My question is answered as one, then two, and then three fuchsia flowers form on what looks like waves of fabric. My mother's scarf! I visualize it as it dances through my mind alive, free, and flowing in the wind. I can still smell the fragrance of her perfume. Although tragic, my mother's death molded my young heart in ways that I am just beginning to understand. For so many years I have been consumed with her loss, and that has blinded me to what lies before me right now. A tear streams down my cheek. Lost and gained. As a little girl, I lost my mother. But that loss is responsible for me finding myself so many years later.

We can all stop pushing now. Are you ready to stop pushing? With constant exertion, can you see why our bodies become sick? With illness and exhaustion, we have no choice but to break when life's drama comes knocking at our doors. It is imperative that we take time to heal the wounds we have incurred in the past. Only then do we have the strength to fully bounce back. I am bouncing back today—flying high in the air like Wonder Woman. I am less concerned about my armor now that I have acknowledged my inner strength.

Grandma called her home God's country. It was her way of showing respect for nature. She always believed that if you cared for nature, it would care for you. After my journey today, I am determined to bounce back from adversity. Reflecting on her words, I realize my error in brushing her words under the carpet. I am listening now. I am writing now. There may be times in our lives when we feel cracked, but there is comfort in knowing we are not broken.

My ball . . . my precious childhood ball completes the canvas today. I observe its graceful elegance as it spins and rocks in the waves of the bay. It is a toy that serves as a symbol of valuable lessons learned. When we see a ball, let it remind us of our inner strength and vitality. Hang a picture of it on the wall if you must. The symbolic ball shall remind us of our resilience and determination and how we are gifted for something powerful. You see, we are peace. We are love. We are light. This realization makes us flexible, fully capable of bending when life pushes on our all-important boundaries. It allows us to resist the urge to break under stress and instead use our experience as a firm foundation—one that lights our inner resolve and catapults us sky-high toward the heavens. As my gaze tracks to the sky, I realize that the darkness in my soul has transitioned into a brilliant rainbow of unimaginable color.

May we all bounce back from adversity and light up the world.

Acknowledgments

I thank all of you.

That's right—everyone. To those who know me well and to the unknown faces who may someday read this book, I am grateful.

Being honest, while writing this book, there were days when my fingers flew across the keyboard eager to express the words in my head. But there were many more days, however, when I was reluctant to write. I would sit crying at my computer, fingers poised over the keyboard, as I attempted to make sense of the emotions that surfaced during the writing process.

I realize now that my hesitation was my subconscious not willing to address painful memories. Writing this book has been therapeutic. It has been the best therapy, and I am stronger for it. I feel liberated and truly free. I can only hope that in reading this book, you will be as well.

Many people worked alongside me to make this book a reality. I would like to extend my heartfelt thanks to all of them.

Jonathan Greer—You are a loving man and incredible husband. I thank God every day for you. You are my rock and are always there when I need you. Thank you for your patience during the many nights I stayed up late writing. You fill my heart with joy each day. I love you, sweetheart.

Mom and Dad—Even in the darkest moments in my life, there was light. That light was you. To this day, I know that if I have a problem,

I can count on you to brighten my day. Through my childhood, you taught me how to be a strong woman who could stand on her own. How incredible I feel to have two parents such as you. I love you both very much.

Trevor, Alexa, and Trace—My babies, my children. You light up my life in more ways than one. You have helped me realize that this is an extraordinary world full of magic, passion, and adventure. You make me feel alive and ready to conquer the world. What an incredible gift. I love you all.

DeLisa Cohen—I feel so blessed to have you as my friend. From childbirth to birthday parties, we have shared so many awesome experiences. You are my biggest cheerleader and always the first to celebrate the successes in my life. You are someone I can always count on. I love you, my friend.

Linda Long—I am truly grateful to have you in my life. When I went from podiatric surgeon to producer to author, you never doubted that I could do it. There were many days when your love and support were the only things that kept me going. I love you for that.

Alan Ebert—I am so proud of who you are. You are a fellow writer, an incredible man, and a beautiful soul. You are my uncle, and I am honored to have you in my life. Your feedback on my writing was invaluable, and I am so grateful. I love you.

Claudia Cano, Jan Killilea, Joanne Duchrow, and Robin Singh—I want you all to know how appreciative I am of your hard work. I have watched you over the years and have learned so much. You inspire me with your courage, drive, and ambition. Thank you for who you are. Love to you all.

Barbara Stewart—It is your creativity and eye for detail that helped shape my vision for this book in the beginning. I feel truly blessed to call you my friend. Thank you for your love and guidance. I love you.

Teri Roberts—You have a heart as big as the world, and it shows in the photographs you take. Thank you for your vision. It shows in the photo on the cover of this book and in my headshots. I appreciate you and all you do. Sending love your way.

Sally Garland—A big thank-you for your editing expertise. What you asked of me required me to reach into deep, dark places in my subconscious to retrieve painful memories. Bringing those memories to light has helped me heal. For that I am grateful. Love to you.

About the Author

DR. SHELLEY PLUMB is a woman on a mission. As a wife, mother, physician, and executive producer at PlumbTalk Productions, she focuses her gifts on uplifting and inspiring others. Born in Renton, Washington, Shelley has always had a life-long love for nature and enjoys hiking, biking, and camping with family and friends.

Adversity came early for Shelley, when at seven years old, she lost her mother in a fatal car accident. She survived the tragedy and has been a living legacy of perseverance ever since. Driven to encourage and energize others, Shelley refuses to let personal trauma define her.

Shelley received her undergraduate degree with honors from Pacific University and went on to earn her doctorate degree from Scholl College of Podiatric Medicine. She served as Chief Podiatry Resident at the prestigious Crozer-Chester Medical Center of Pennsylvania, where she completed her podiatric surgical training.

Moving to West Palm Beach, Florida, Shelley built a thriving podiatric surgical practice. While her professional career was in full swing she gave birth to three beautiful children—an experience she considers to be one of her highest honors. As her career became increasingly demanding, Shelley struggled with work–life balance, finding it difficult to juggle the demands of her profession and three small children under the age of five. She found herself alone, confused, and exhausted, as her marriage disintegrated and the heartbreak of divorce led to yet another defining moment in her life.

One morning, in the midst of the divorce process, Shelley sat in her bedroom staring out the window. Her mind cried out, *What are you going to do?* Her heart replied, *You can either let your life spiral down and out of control or you can turn your pain into something productive.* That morning, she put a pen to paper. On the left side of the paper, she set to work writing down the specific reasons why she was unhappy. On the right side of the paper, she proceeded to write everything she could do to change her situation—and her life. That brainstorm session led to an outline, a draft, and finally a business plan for PlumbTalk Productions—a multi-media production company she now operates out of West Palm Beach, Florida.

As the founder, CEO, and executive producer at Plumb Talk Productions, Shelley provides worldwide state-of-the-art video production services for businesses. She assists individuals in achieving their lifelong ambitions through increased exposure and the power of video marketing. She is revered in her professional community for her creativity and attention to detail. Shelley is said by many to "put the heart back in video production."

Empowering individuals is something Shelley excels at. Under the umbrella of PlumbTalk Productions, Shelley has developed a revolutionary speaker support program called Standing Ovation. Through the Standing Ovation program, Shelley is honored to coach, manage, and promote some of the most inspiring, motivational speakers in South Florida. Through this state-of-the-art program, Shelley is driven to give speakers the support they deserve.

It was not an easy transition from physician to entrepreneur, but with the support of her family, friends, children, and loving second husband, Shelley continues to thrive as a producer, video coach, and prominent speaker. Forever thankful for the competent team at PlumbTalk Productions, Shelley is the embodiment of a renaissance woman, uplifting and empowering others through her words and actions.

One of Shelley's favorite quotes states, "Reach out, so you will begin seeing what is within."

This statement is the embodiment of Shelley's own philosophy, as she continually challenges herself to rise above adversity and to see beyond her current state. Through life's journey as a wife, mother, and entrepreneur, Shelley firmly believes that individuals who feel good about themselves feels empowered—and empowered individuals empower society.

Empowered she is. There was a moment in her life when Shelley had lost sight of who she was. Shelley has not only discovered a career that sings to her soul, but she is thrilled to spend quality time with her family and friends. Through adversity and success alike, Shelley feels as if she has found the greatest treasure of all—*she has finally found herself.*